Sustainable Cities

A Simple Guide for Everyone

Nova Martian

Disclaimer

This book has been created with the assistance of AI tools for content generation, editing, and formatting. While
AI tools have contributed to its development, the content has been reviewed to ensure its quality and accuracy.
Readers are encouraged to approach the material critically and verify information where necessary.

Contents

Introduction

The twenty-first century marks an era of unprecedented urbanization, where more than half of the world's population resides in cities. As engines of economic growth and innovation, cities act as critical hubs for culture, education, and development. However, this rapid urban expansion brings forth unique challenges that encompass environmental degradation, resource depletion, and social inequities. The concept of sustainable cities emerges as a crucial paradigm to address these challenges and to foster urban environments that are not only livable and resilient but also equitable and harmonious with nature.

This book, "Sustainable Cities: A Simple Guide for Everyone," endeavors to offer a comprehensive understanding of what constitutes a sustainable city and the essential components that drive its realization. It aims to unravel the complexities surrounding urban sustainability and translate them into practical and accessible knowledge for readers from all walks of life. Sustainability is not just an abstract idea but a pragmatic approach that involves rethinking how cities are planned, built, and governed. It invites us to envision urban spaces that prioritize the well-being of their inhabitants while ensuring the health of our planet.

In the spirit of fostering an inclusive dialogue, this book covers a spectrum of topics integral to shaping sustainable urban futures. Each chapter delves into core aspects such as urban planning, energy efficiency, transportation, community engagement, and governance. The topics are carefully curated to provide a foundational understanding of the principles and practices that contribute to making cities sustainable. Through real-world examples and case studies, the book illustrates how cities around the globe are implementing innovative solutions to achieve sustainability goals.

As we navigate through these chapters, the book emphasizes the importance of collaboration and collective action. The transformation towards sustainable cities requires the concerted efforts of policymakers, planners, businesses, and, crucially, the community. It necessitates a recognition of the interconnectedness of economic, social, and environmental systems. By providing insights into various strategies and models, this book seeks to inspire actionable change and encourage readers to take part in the broader discourse on urban sustainability.

In conclusion, as we look towards the future, it is imperative to approach urban development with sustainability at its core. The sustainable city is not merely an aspiration but an achievable goal that demands our attention and dedication. Through understanding and implementing the concepts discussed in "Sustainable Cities: A Simple Guide for Everyone," we can work towards creating urban environments that nurture our communities and safeguard our natural world, ensuring prosperity for current and future generations.

Chapter 1

Introduction to Sustainable Cities

Sustainable cities are urban areas designed with a focus on ecological balance, social equity, and economic viability. This chapter explores the evolution of urban sustainability, identifies key components of a sustainable city, and addresses challenges cities face in becoming sustainable. It also highlights successful examples from around the world, demonstrating practical approaches to achieving urban sustainability while enhancing the quality of life for all residents.

1.1   Understanding Sustainable Development

Sustainable development is a term often thrown around in discussions about the future of our cities, countries, and indeed, our planet. But what does it really mean, especially when translated to the bustling realms of urban environments? To truly grasp the essence and significance of sustainable development, it's vital to travel back in time to its roots and then return armed with new insights to the modern metropolis.

The story of sustainable development formally begins in 1987 with the release of the Brundtland Report, also known as "Our Common Future." Published by the World Commission on Environment and Development, this pivotal document provided the most frequently cited definition of sustainable development: "development that meets the needs of the present without compromising the ability of future generations to meet their own needs." This deceptively simple statement encapsulates a complex balance of economic growth, environmental stewardship, and social equity.

Urban environments are where this balance becomes most critical and challenging.   Cities are dynamic ecosystems, humming with human activity and acting as both problem areas and solutions in the quest for sustainability.   With more than half of the world's population now residing in urban areas—a percentage expected to rise—cities are at the front lines of resource consumption and pollution, yet they also serve as the crucibles of innovation and progressive policy-making.

The practice of sustainable development in urban contexts revolves around three core pillars: environmental integrity, economic viability, and social equity. Each one plays an integral role in shaping cities that are livable now, as well as into the future.

Environmental Integrity: Building Resilience amid Concrete

Imagine an urban landscape where green spaces are as ubiquitous as the skyline dotted with skyscrapers. This vision reflects the environmental pillar of sustainable development, which emphasizes not merely the preservation of existing natural resources, but their integration and enhancement within cityscapes. Urban planners face the formidable task of replenishing green spaces that promote biodiversity, converting abandoned land to tamed habitats or recreational parks, and developing infrastructure that minimizes ecological footprints. This approach often takes the form of green roofs, urban farms, and intricate networks of public transportation designed to reduce reliance on fossil fuels.

Implementing strategies that harness renewable energy is equally vital. Solar panels converting sunlight into energy on the rooftops of downtown buildings, wind turbines adorning the peripheries, and innovative wastewater systems symbolize progress — not just conservation. This isn't simply about saving trees but rather acknowledging our capacity to alter natural resources sustainably in and around cities.

Economic Viability: Wealth in a Wise Economy

Turning to the economic viability of a sustainable city, we uncover a narrative driven by efficiency and innovation. Sustainable development rejects the notion of economic growth as inherently opposed to environmental health; instead, it frames a flourishing economy as one that recognizes and harnesses the potential for resource efficiency. This paradigm promotes green businesses and sustainable markets, screens for low-carbon technologies, and encourages business models that recycle and renew.

Consider modern cities that have championed investment in sustainable infrastructure — building roads, bridges, and sewer systems that, while initially expensive, promise lower long-term costs through durability and energy savings. Moreover, these infrastructure improvements can stimulate jobs and economic opportunities, particularly in new sectors related to sustainability, thus marrying the market forces with environmentally sound practices for community growth.

Social Equity: Bridging the Urban Divides

Social equity within urban sustainable development is the bridge that connects the other two pillars, ensuring that the benefits of a sustainable city are delicately yet profoundly dispersed among its population. Sustainable urban environments must not only be environmentally sound and economically vibrant, but they must also be fair, inclusive, and equitable.

A glimpse into social equity unveils endeavors like affordable housing programs, equitable access to public services, and policies that encourage community involvement and ownership in urban planning decisions. When all residents, irrespective of income, have access to essentials such as clean air, water, education, and health services, they contribute positively to urban life. Furthermore, socially equitable practices in urban areas can alleviate disparities, reducing poverty and its associated challenges.

Practical examples abound from cities stepping up to this sustainability challenge. Copenhagen exemplifies bicycling successes with over 50% of its population commuting to work on bikes, thereby reducing emissions and fostering a healthier lifestyle. Curitiba in Brazil has pioneered sophisticated, efficient public transport systems as an answer to the growing demands of urban mobility, proving both environmentally and economically beneficial.

In tackling the social dimension, Singapore's focus on public housing shows how cities can design inclusive communities by integrating schools, leisure areas, and local businesses, ensuring affordable living options for its diverse population.

The Ultimate Goal: An Urban Symphony

Achieving sustainable development in an urban environment is akin to conducting an intricate symphony. It's not just about hitting all the right notes — economic, ecological, and social — but about ensuring these notes harmonize, creating a beautiful, long-lasting melody. Cities of the future, which are being shaped today through conscientious urban planning and investment, stand poised as examples of how humanity can thrive within planetary boundaries.

The importance of sustainable development in urban areas extends beyond mere survival — it's an active blueprint for nurturing flourishing, resilient communities that can adapt to changes and innovations over time. By embedding these principles within the DNA of townships, cities unlock opportunities that promise a richer, more resilient urban life for present and future generations.

In our urban future, as we weave sustainability through every fiber of city living, not only do we safeguard the essence of our environment and economy, but we continue the timeless endeavor of building places that honor humanity's innate connection to the earth and each other. Such is the essence of sustainable development — a guiding light amid the dark uncertainties of tomorrow's urban life.

1.2 The Evolution of Urban Sustainability

The journey toward urban sustainability is a tale rich with transformative ideas and groundbreaking changes. From ancient cities to modern metropolises, the seeds of sustainable practices have been sown, watered, and now stand on the brink of a future that promises innovation at an unprecedented scale.   Exploring this evolution provides a lens through which we grasp the intricacies of sustainable urbanism, chart its progression, and envision what lies ahead.

Let's start by traveling back in time before "urban sustainability" was a term slapped on research papers and policy agendas.   Picture the Roman Empire at the height of its power: a sprawling network of cities knit together by aqueducts, subterranean sewers, and roads, showcasing early feats in sustainable urban planning.   These innovations were as much about survival as they were about sophistication.   However, the intentions behind such infrastructures—though not labeled sustainable—were clear: support growing populations, manage resources efficiently, and mitigate disease.

Fast forward to the Industrial Revolution, an era that redefined urban living with its great leaps in technology but equally great leaps in pollution and resource exploitation.   Cities expanded rapidly, and the degradation of the urban environment became an alarming consequence of unchecked industrialization. It was a period of learning, albeit through trials and considerable errors, that unchecked growth without regard for environmental repercussions simply wasn't tenable.

It wasn't until the mid-20th century that urban sustainability began to crystallize as a formal concept. Post-World War II reconstruction led to urban expansion that, while advantageous, also forced cities to reckon with burgeoning populations, pollution, and traffic-congested streets.   The visible consequences of urban sprawl sparked a response—a push to rethink how cities could grow more organically alongside nature rather than against it.

The environmental movement of the 1960s and 1970s laid additional groundwork, emphasizing the plight of natural ecosystems at risk from human activity. Books like Rachel Carson's "Silent Spring," though primarily focused on rural and natural environments, stirred public and political consciousness toward the environmental costs of development. Cities, as hubs of progress, became focal points for this growing awareness.

The latter part of the 20th century introduced pivotal frameworks promoting urban sustainability. In 1972, the United Nations Conference on the Human Environment—often referred to as the Stockholm Conference—marked the first large-scale recognition of environmental issues on the international stage, setting the stage for later, more vigorous global commitments.

As policymakers and urbanists grappled with escalating environmental concerns, milestones were reached in adopting sustainability principles. By the 1990s, Local Agenda 21, an action plan from the Rio Earth Summit responding to sustainable development, became a beacon guiding many city planners and administrators. This guide emphasized local action as the linchpin in achieving global sustainability objectives.

Parallel to political and academic shifts, technology became an ally in sculpting sustainable urban environments. Information technology and emerging fields like geospatial analysis enabled urban planners to model impacts, forecast growth, and plan infrastructure with greater precision and less waste. The dialogue between technology and urbanism spawned the "smart city" concept—a foray into harnessing data and connectivity for managing urban services sustainably.

Today, innovative practices and principles are deeply

woven into the fabric of urban development. Cities like Amsterdam inspire with their extensive cycling infrastructure and progressive energy policies, serving as models for how urban environments can thrive with minimized climate impact. Meanwhile, Curitiba remains a paragon of efficient public transportation, having streamlined bus systems to reduce congestion and encourage sustainable commutes.

As we pivot toward the future, the trajectory of urban sustainability faces dynamic challenges and opportunities. The integration of renewable energy technologies—solar panels seamlessly integrating into building designs, wind farms coexisting with urban landscapes—represents a growing trend in marrying renewable capabilities with urban expansion. The rise of the urban agriculture movement is breathing new life into neglected spaces, transforming rooftops and vacant lots into sources of local, nutritious food.

The next horizon hints at a paradigm shift harnessing the power of circular economies within urban contexts. Imagine a city where waste is considered a resource— a place where consumption and production cycles are meticulously managed to eliminate redundancy and pollution. This vision, however idealistic, underscores the mindset required for continuous urban sustainability advancement.

As urban populations continue to swell, so does the responsibility to innovate sustainably. Engaging communities as contributors rather than mere stakeholders in city planning could lead to breakthroughs in participative governance and nurtured urban biodiversity.

At the heart of urban sustainability's evolution is the understanding that cities must dynamically balance growth, innovation, and conservation—a balancing act steered by the relentless pursuit of harmony between humanity and its urban creations. This evolution may not always be linear, but its trajectory is firmly set on a course towards cities that are not just smarter and more efficient, but deeply considerate of their environmental and social footprints. By leveraging the lessons of the past and the tools of the present, urban landscapes are poised to lead the charge into a sustainable future with bold confidence.

1.3 Key Components of a Sustainable City

Picture a city where nature and the built environment coalesce into a harmonious urban symphony. This is not the stuff of fantasy, but of sustainable urban design, a practice that transforms cities into nurturing habitats for both people and the planet. What, then, are the secret ingredients—the key components—that blend together to create this symphony of sustainability?

Green Infrastructure: Nature's Urban Ally

At the heart of sustainable cities lies green infrastructure, a term that evokes imagery of verdant rooftops and tree-lined streets. Green infrastructure doesn't simply greenify our surroundings; it serves multifaceted roles in urban sustainability. Trees and parks work as the city's lungs, absorbing carbon and expelling oxygen while reducing the urban heat island effect. Well-placed vegetation can cool cities in summer, cutting energy consumption in air conditioning and fostering habitats for urban biodiversity.

Consider Tokyo's dedication to maintaining open spaces: the integration of public parks and green belts showcases how expansive urban parks can improve air quality and mental well-being. In densely populated cities like New York, Central Park isn't just an iconic retreat but a crucial ecological and social asset—a living testament to the critical role of green spaces in sustainable urban landscapes.

Efficient and Reliable Public Transportation: The City's Circulatory System

Efficient public transportation is another cornerstone of a sustainable city, akin to the efficient circulatory system of a healthy body. Public transport networks integrated with pedestrian pathways and cycling lanes promote mobility while reducing carbon emissions. Cities like Zurich and Singapore have made public transportation an art form: their systems are not just alternative modes of travel, but the primary ones for many residents. The benefits go beyond emissions reductions; less car reliance means reduced traffic congestion, improved public health, and more vibrant communities.

Renewable Energy Integration: Powering the Future

Evolving from globalization's industrial roots, energy use is ubiquitous, thus reforming its production is paramount for sustainability. Cities poised for the future exhibit storied commitment to cutting-edge renewable energy solutions. Wind turbines, solar arrays, and tidal systems knit a renewable tapestry, weaving energy into the urban grid. Cities from San Francisco to Copenhagen have committed to achieving carbon neutrality, with renewables as their weapon of choice. The lesson: the energy feeding a sustainable city must be as clean and as renewable as possible to ensure longevity without detriments to the natural environment.

Waste Management: The Art of Urban Alchemy

Sustainable urban dwellers transform what others may consider detritus into resources. Balancing consumption with thoughtful waste management practices is a crucial step toward harmonizing urban living with the planet's finite resources. In Vienna, cutting-edge waste management transforms residual refuse into district heating. Meanwhile, San Francisco's Zero Waste initiative seeks to eliminate landfill waste entirely by 2025, relying on recycling, composting, and innovative waste-to-resource conversions. These dynamic strategies manifest the tenet of reduce, reuse, and recycle in daily life, proving that one person's trash can indeed be another's treasure.

Water Management: Navigating the Urban Blue

Managing water resources wisely is another key component, especially as the climate crisis escalates. The elixir of life itself must be managed meticulously in sustainable cities, with demand outpacing supply. Sustainable urban water practices often merge old-world wisdom with new-age technology. The ancient qanat systems of the Middle East serve as early examples of sustainable water management, channeling groundwater through gravity-fed tunnels to cultivated lands. In modern cities like Amsterdam, smart water metering and green rooftops mitigate flash floods, unlocking resilience as cities face weather extremes.

Sustainable Housing: Building Community Foundations

Architecture and housing studies reveal that sustainable urban living isn't solely about technology but also about connecting communities through sustainable design. Housing must adapt, blend, and persist alongside natural surroundings, ensuring affordability and accessibility remain core principles. The practice

13

extends beyond energy-efficient buildings into collective housing solutions known as co-housing, which leverage shared resources to reduce footprints and foster community bonds.   In the heart of eco-towns like Freiburg (Germany), solar panels rationalize roof space, and prefabricated materials redefine building justice. Sustainable housing embodies urban sustainability not through skyscraper-size alone but through lifestyle-focused design.

Encouraging Local Economies: Thriving Within City Borders

Finally, sustainable cities support local economies, embodying resilience by reducing dependency and amplifying regional strengths. Encouragement arises through markets glowing with local produce, artisanal shops resonating with community spirit, and economies embracing circular principles. Cities like Portland in the United States pursue prosperity via buy-local movements, while Barcelona prioritizes cooperative economies. Anchored in community and synergy, local economies drive sustainable cities as centers of diverse industry innovation because they root financial health in social and environmental stewardship.

In sum, these key components function not in isolation but as a synergy, building a city's structure upon sustainability's triad: ecological health, economic vitality, and social equity. Unlike mythical utopias, these elements reflect a series of conscious choices—from codified policies to grassroots movements.   Through these urban symphonies, we chart an evolving course toward a new dawn, alive with a thriving, sustainable future.

1.4 Challenges to Achieving Urban Sustainability

As enchanting as the vision of a sustainable city may be, getting there is akin to navigating a labyrinth filled with formidable obstacles. From political to practical, and economic to environmental, the challenges that lie in the path of urban sustainability are both numerous and intricate. Yet, like daring adventurers, cities across the globe continue to push forward, determined to untangle these knots and carve sustainable futures.

Let's start with the beast of *competing priorities*. Cities are bustling entities with enormous responsibilities and limited resources. On one hand, there's the pressing need to address immediate issues like unemployment, housing shortages, and public health. On the other hand, there are crucial sustainability goals such as lowering carbon emissions, increasing green spaces, and revamping transportation. Juggling these priorities often places sustainable initiatives in the precarious position of being shelved or underfunded, as urgent short-term needs scream louder than long-term sustainability whispers.

The challenge unveils itself starkly in budgetary meetings where funding for new bus networks, solar installations, or urban gardens must compete with the repair of existing infrastructures or emergency services. The key lies in urban planners' ability to align sustainability endeavors with economic and social objectives, showing how they can contribute to immediate civic problems through job creation, energy savings, and improved quality of life.

Socioeconomic inequalities represent another critical hurdle. Urban sustainability thrives on equitable access to resources, yet the staggering disparities within city

15

landscapes often mean that benefits are not evenly distributed.   Low-income areas frequently reside in less green, more polluted neighborhoods, cut off from the sustainable advantages found in wealthier districts. This divide demonstrates how socioeconomic inequality can thwart sustainability goals, posing the question: how can cities build consensus and engagement without leaving significant swathes of the population behind?

Take, for example, the fate of low-income communities in rapidly gentrifying cities. While some areas celebrate new sustainable infrastructure, residents soon face rising living costs, leading to displacement.   Sustainability must avoid becoming a harbinger of new inequalities by proactively engaging all community sectors in planning and decision-making efforts, fostering inclusivity and shared ownership.

Closely intertwined with social challenges is the *political landscape*, a charged terrain where urban sustainability can become a ping-pong ball in policy debates. Changes in political leadership and priorities can stall or derail environmental agendas, as policies set by one administration may be cast aside by the next. This lack of continuity creates uncertainty for long-term urban projects, dissuading investment and challenging proactive solutions.   Cities need strong civic coalitions and nonpartisan momentum to anchor sustainability securely beyond electoral cycles.

Imagine the plight of electric vehicle infrastructure projects launched by a progressive legislature, only to witness their funding yanked by a subsequent political windswing. Here lies a key challenge: fostering collaborative governance models and bureaucratic resilience to safeguard urban sustainability against the tremors of political change.

One cannot explore the path to urban sustainability without encountering the *technological gap*. While innovations continue to expand possibilities, the digital and infrastructure divide between cities can magnify other challenges. Emerging technologies in smart grids, renewable energy, and water management require significant upfront investment and expertise, causing less affluent cities to lag behind their counterparts.

For instance, Tokyo's revered bullet trains run on advanced technology and sustainable practices, but they starkly contrast with cities grappling to upgrade aged public transportation. Bridging this gap demands strategic alliances and knowledge-sharing networks that enable cities worldwide to access sustainable innovations regardless of economic stature, ensuring no urban center is left lurking in the shadows of advancement.

Then, there's the looming specter of *climate change*, amplifying challenges and threatening the very progress cities strive to achieve. Climate impacts—rising sea levels, increasing temperatures, and erratic weather patterns—magnify existing urban problems, pushing systems to their limits. The cost to fortify cities against these changes is enormous, demanding that urban planners embed resilience within the urban fabric to withstand nature's unpredictability while curbing cities' contributions to climate change.

Consider the plight of coastal cities like Miami, fighting against encroaching sea levels with each tide—a vivid illustration of nature dictating urban challenges. For them, sustainability morphs from aspiration to necessity, but it comes with a hefty price tag. Innovation must evolve faster than nature's adversities, prompting cities to invest in multi-functional infrastructures that enhance their adaptive capacities.

As if staring at an unsolvable puzzle, *behavioral inertia* looms as one of the most intricate barriers of all. Citizen behavior and lifestyle choices are linchpins in the successful adoption of sustainability practices. Yet ingrained habits can resist change, entrenched by a comfort zone that clings to convenience. Shifting societal behavior for sustainability demands deep cultural change— an undertaking that requires time, patience, and creativity.

Take the simple act of adopting recycling habits. For environmentally conscious cities, a fundamental challenge lies in embedding these habits universally— beyond motivated communities to every household, each consumer, and all industries. School programs, incentives, and awareness campaigns are primed to dismantle inertia, turning sustainability into shared practice, not just policy.

Ultimately, achieving urban sustainability presents a series of complex trade-offs and adaptations. These challenges are not insurmountable impediments; rather, they offer opportunities for innovation, collaboration, and imaginative problem-solving. Cities, as ecosystems at the nexus of human civilization, must navigate these intricate challenges with foresight, ensuring their ascendancy toward sustainability is a tale of resilience and creativity—a legacy for generations yet to come.

1.5   Success Stories and Case Studies

In the world of urban development, few stories captivate as much as those of cities successfully navigating the journey toward sustainability. These urban centers are living laboratories where ideas are tested, stretched, and sometimes miraculously transformed into new norms.

Let's explore some of these cities that have surged to the forefront of sustainability, providing both inspiration and blueprints for others to follow.

Start with **Copenhagen**, a city synonymous with environmental foresight, consistently ranking as one of the world's greenest metropolises. Known for its cycling culture, Copenhagen's streets are woven with over 390 kilometers of bike lanes, serving as arteries for its eco-conscious populace. The city has nurtured this mode of transport through policy initiatives dating back to the 1970s—policies that grew from the energy crises which forced a reevaluation of car dependency. Today, around 62% of Copenhageners commute to work or school by bike. This isn't just a statistic; it represents a collective commitment to cutting carbon emissions and reducing urban congestion while improving public health.

But Copenhagen's quest for sustainability doesn't halt at pedal-powered commutes. It's also ambitiously aiming to become the world's first carbon-neutral city by 2025. Energy-efficient urban projects pepper the city's landscape, underpinned by wind power and district heating systems that recycle energy from incinerated waste. The integration of renewable energy into every facet of urban life has helped ground the city as a pioneer of sustainable transformation.

Next, journey to **Curitiba** in Brazil, a city often hailed as a paragon of public transport innovation. In the 1970s, Curitiba faced rapid urban population growth, conjuring images of future chaos. Yet, with far-sighted urban planning led by then-mayor Jaime Lerner, the city adopted the Bus Rapid Transit (BRT) system. This system, characterized by dedicated lanes and tubular stations allowing advance payment, greatly reduced travel times and made buses a preferred travel mode, reflecting nearly one million daily passengers.

This strategic shift demonstrates how cities can forge sustainable paths through transportation redesign, tackling challenges like air pollution and traffic congestion head-on.   Curitiba's urban planning emphasized a holistic approach, intertwining access to green spaces and comprehensive waste management, establishing an environment where sustainability thrives in tandem with growth.

Swing your compass to **Singapore**, a leader in integrating nature within its urban jungle. As a city-state punctuated by dense populations and tall skyscrapers, Singapore's transformation into a "City in a Garden" was deliberate, driven by biophilic design principles and meticulous urban planning. Integrating nature into architecture and planning—seen in buildings adorned with vertical gardens, renewable energy-powered rainwater gardens, and interconnected park systems—demonstrates the city's commitment to creating an urban space inherently in tune with nature.

Furthermore, Singapore's water management prowess is legendary. Lacking natural water resources, the city has crafted a sophisticated strategy involving rainwater catchment, desalinated water, and a comprehensive network of reservoirs. These innovations have mitigated water scarcity concerns, showing that geographical challenges can become opportunities for revolutionary advancements.

Beyond Asia, **Portland, Oregon**, stands out in the United States for its environmental stewardship, boasting accolades as one of America's most sustainable cities. The city has curtailed suburban sprawl through strict zoning laws and the establishment of urban growth boundaries to protect surrounding farmland

and forests. Portland's vision underscores sustainability through urban density, where vibrant communities flourish with walkable neighborhoods and green public transport systems, relying on an active cycling community and efficient light rail networks.

Portland's devotion to renewable energy is noteworthy, with clean energy now accounting for a substantial portion of the city's power supply. This, together with community efforts in urban farming and green building initiatives, fosters an ecosystem of sustainability practices influencing other North American cities.

Finally, let's venture to **Stockholm**, celebrating its image as a "European Green Capital." Boasting an extensive network of public transport options, overground and underground trains are harmonized seamlessly with bus and light rail systems, making car-free commuting accessible and favorable. But Stockholm's sustainability laurels extend beyond transportation.

The city has earned global praise for its Hammarby Sjöstad district—a futuristic residential quarter designed around sustainability principles from its inception. This district raises the bar on urban living, with buildings built to high energy efficiency standards, waste heat recycled for water treatment, and non-combustible waste converted into district heating. Such holistic urban planning serves as a prototype for sustainable developments worldwide.

While these cities illuminate the path to sustainability through varying approaches and priorities, their common thread lies in the vision and commitment to pursuing extraordinary innovations. They provide blueprints, yes—not to be copied, but to be adapted, translated, and transformed to address unique challenges facing cities worldwide.

Ultimately, the success stories of these cities are not accomplishments in isolation. They reflect the art of crafting sustainable environments that nurture growth while preserving equity and the planet's resources. Each represents a canvas painted with ingenuity, demonstrating that while the challenges of creating sustainable cities are immense, so too are the possibilities when communities, technology, and policy combine in visionary harmony. These cities' feats inspire us all to think differently about the places we inhabit and to dream expansively about the sustainable legacies we can leave behind.

Chapter 2

The Importance of Urban Sustainability

Urban sustainability is crucial due to growing populations and environmental impacts of cities. This chapter examines how sustainable practices enhance economic resilience, improve public health, and promote social equity. It underscores the need for reducing environmental footprints while supporting vibrant urban economies, and includes methodologies for measuring sustainability achievements within urban areas. This approach ensures cities remain livable, inclusive, and capable of meeting future challenges effectively.

2.1   The Growing Urban Population

In 1800, a mere 3% of the world's population resided in urban areas. Fast forward to today, over half of humanity lives in cities, a proportion that is projected to soar to nearly 70% by 2050. This seismic shift from rural to urban living has been one of the most significant demographic transformations in human history, and understanding its nuances is crucial for fostering sustainable urban development.

The magnetic pull of cities can be attributed to several factors. Historically, cities have been epicenters of economic opportunities. They offer jobs, better living standards, and access to education, healthcare, and cultural amenities. The Industrial Revolution served as a catalyst, drawing populations from rural regions to urban centers with the promise of prosperity and social mobility. Modern technology and globalization have only amplified this urban allure, transforming cities into international hubs of activity and innovation.

However, as the urban landscape expands, so do its complex challenges. The unprecedented rate of urban growth presents acute implications for sustainability. Cities must now grapple with increasing demands for energy, water, and waste management, all while striving to minimize their ecological footprint.   As concrete jungles replace green spaces, the environmental, social, and economic foundations of urban living require careful reconsideration to ensure livable, resilient communities for the future.

Yet, not all cities are expanding at the same pace or in the same manner. Mega-cities, defined as urban areas surpassing 10 million inhabitants, coexist alongside rapidly growing mid-sized and smaller cities.   While cities like Tokyo, New York, and Delhi represent much of the urbanization narrative, it is places like Lagos, Dar es Salaam, and Jakarta that epitomize the explosive urban growth forecasted to dominate the 21st century.

Urbanization brings both opportunities and challenges to the forefront. On one hand, denser human settlements can lead to more efficient use of resources. For instance, urban environments encourage the development of public transportation networks, potentially reducing reliance on individual vehicles and cutting greenhouse gas emissions.   However, unchecked and poorly planned urban sprawl can lead to sprawling slums, transportation gridlock, and heightened pollution levels, negating these potential benefits.

The line between prosperity and sustainability sometimes blurs. Cities are hotbeds of economic activity, producing over 80% of global GDP. Nevertheless, they are also significant contributors to global carbon emissions and resource depletion, consuming more than two-thirds of the world's energy. The dilemma then becomes one of balancing growth with the imperative to minimize environmental harm—a challenge that underscores the need for innovative urban planning and infrastructure design.

As cities burgeon, the housing dilemma is increasingly pronounced. Approximately one billion people live in informal settlements or slums, often without access to basic services such as clean water, sanitation, and secure tenure. This disparity poses serious risks to social cohesion and public health, emphasizing the necessity for inclusive urban policies that cater to diverse populations while promoting equity.

Interestingly, the concept of "smart cities" emerges as a beacon of hope in addressing these multifaceted challenges. Leveraging technology and data, smart cities aim to enhance the quality of urban life, optimize the use of resources, and create efficient environments responsive to the needs of their citizens. Solutions range from smart grids managing electricity more effectively to urban farming initiatives that bring food production closer to consumers, reducing the carbon footprint of food distribution.

Moreover, the urban population growth intersects with global trends like climate change and technological advancement. As sea levels rise and extreme weather events become more frequent, cities located on coastlines or in vulnerable geographies face increased risks.

Conversely, advances in technology provide the tools to model, predict, and mitigate these environmental impacts.

Population growth also demands a rethinking of how urban spaces are structured. Mixed-use developments that combine residential, commercial, and recreational spaces can reduce the need for long commutes, thus cutting emissions and enhancing community connectivity. Furthermore, increased green spaces, such as parks and green roofs, not only beautify urban environments but also serve crucial ecological functions by absorbing rainwater and lowering urban heat effects.

Education and social innovation play pivotal roles too. Educating urban dwellers about sustainable practices can catalyze grassroots movements towards greener living. Community-driven initiatives often hold the power to effect significant change, fostering sustainable behaviors across diverse urban populations.

The rapid upward trajectory of urban population growth requires critical reflection and proactive measures to ensure sustainable and inclusive development. The goal is not simply to accommodate more people but to craft urban environments where quality of life is paramount, communities thrive, and ecological limits are respected. As cities continue to expand their reach, the mandate is clear: to harness the forces of urbanization towards creating flourishing, sustainable habitats capable of supporting future generations.

2.2   Environmental Impact of Urban Areas

Cities, the bustling metropolises where humanity's greatest achievements and challenges intersect, hold the key to our environmental future. Though occupying only about 3% of the Earth's land, urban areas are responsible for a staggering 70% of global carbon dioxide emissions and consume over two-thirds of the world's energy. This disproportionate impact underscores the pressing need for urban sustainability. To comprehend the full scope of urban environmental impact, we must unravel the layers of this complex relationship between city life and ecological health.

Let us begin with one of the most conspicuous facets of urban life: air pollution. The narratives of many cities are written in the smog that envelopes their skylines. From vehicles spewing exhaust to industrial plants releasing pollutants, air quality in urban areas often suffers. Particulate matter (PM), nitrogen dioxide, and sulfur dioxide are common culprits, leading to health issues ranging from respiratory problems to heart disease. Cities like Beijing and Delhi have become infamous for their air quality crises, yet these issues are surprisingly ubiquitous, affecting urban areas worldwide.

The ramifications extend beyond human health. Airborne pollutants can lead to acid rain, damaging ecosystems, reducing biodiversity, and altering soil and water chemistry. In a twisted irony, cities—intended as centers of life—can become vectors of harm to the natural environment that surrounds and supports them.

Urban areas also dramatically reshape the natural landscape. The proliferation of concrete, asphalt, and steel promotes the "urban heat island" effect, where cities become significantly warmer than their rural counterparts. This phenomenon is not merely an inconvenience; it exacerbates the demand for air conditioning, leading to higher energy consumption and further carbon emissions. Moreover, the heat can exacerbate pollution, as high temperatures increase the concentrations of ground-level ozone.

Water management presents another monumental challenge. Urbanization, with its extensive networks of paved surfaces, disrupts natural water cycles. Rainwater, rather than seeping into the ground to replenish aquifers, is rapidly diverted into storm systems, increasing the risk of flooding. In 2021, dramatic images of inundated subway stations in New York and Zhengzhou highlighted how unprepared many cities are for increasingly intense precipitation events—ironically, sometimes exacerbated by climate change, another issue compounded by urban activities.

Moreover, urban runoff often carries pollutants into waterways, impairing aquatic ecosystems and threatening wildlife. This pollution alters habitats, affecting the health and diversity of species from amphibians to fish. The demand for water itself in cities can deplete local and distant water resources, sometimes diverting water from essential ecological zones and agricultural needs.

The built environment in cities, while iconic and architecturally impressive, contributes to resource depletion. The construction and maintenance of infrastructure require vast amounts of raw materials, like metals, timber, and sand. Urban expansion thus feeds into global supply chains that can lead to deforestation, habitat loss, and other forms of environmental degradation.

Our waste-disposal habits in cities compound these issues. Landfills, often situated near urban areas, are more than just mounds of refuse. They are complex bioreactors producing methane, a potent greenhouse gas. The challenge of waste management grows with urban populations, necessitating more sustainable solutions such as recycling and composting to mitigate these impacts.

Sustainability in urban environments is, therefore, not a mere option but a necessity. Strategies to lessen urban environmental impacts embrace diverse fields and innovative thinking. Green architecture, for instance, has gained ground, with buildings increasingly designed to reduce energy consumption through better insulation, solar panels, and efficient HVAC systems. The rise of "living buildings," those that give back more than they take, suggests a promising frontier for urban sustainability.

Transportation, traditionally a significant contributor to air pollution, is undergoing a revolution. The push towards electric vehicles (EVs), enhanced public transportation, and infrastructure for bicycles and pedestrians aims to reduce urban reliance on fossil fuels. Cities like Amsterdam and Copenhagen provide leading examples of how cycling can be integrated into the fabric of urban life, offering health and environmental benefits.

Urban planning also plays an instrumental role. By prioritizing green spaces, cities can mitigate the urban heat island effect, promote biodiversity, and improve the quality of life for residents. Green roofs, urban forests, and parks are not just aesthetic features; they are vital components of urban ecosystems that offer shade, absorb carbon dioxide, and support wildlife.

Climate resilience is becoming a central theme in urban policy as well, with cities incorporating adaptive strategies to withstand environmental stressors. Flood defenses, such as those in Rotterdam, and innovative drainage solutions, seen in Singapore's integration of water-sensitive urban design, exemplify how cities can prepare for an uncertain climate future.

While cities are hubs of innovation and economic

activity, they are also at the forefront of environmental impact. Urban sustainability requires a multifaceted approach, weaving together technology, policy, and community engagement to create livable and resilient urban environments. By addressing the environmental pitfalls inherent in urbanization, cities can transform from sources of ecological strain into beacons of sustainable development, leading the global charge against climate change and environmental decline.

2.3 Economic Benefits of Sustainable Cities

Cities today, more than ever, are the bustling heartbeats of global economic activity. Yet, while they account for the lion's share of the world's wealth, their rhythms are often out of sync with sustainability. The challenge here is more than an environmental one; it's fundamentally economic. This isn't just about ensuring cleaner air or prettier parks—important as those are—but about recognizing that embedding sustainability within urban frameworks can vastly enhance economic performance. Contrary to traditional beliefs that green equates to expensive, sustainable cities are proving to be hubs of economic vitality and resilience, offering an array of tangible benefits that ripple beyond their boundaries.

Embracing sustainability turns cities into magnets for innovation and investment. Businesses today recognize the importance of sustainable practices as both a responsibility and a strategic advantage. The allure of sustainability attracts forward-thinking companies that offer innovative solutions to urban challenges—creating jobs and bolstering local economies. Firms pioneering in renewable energy, waste management, and sustainable architecture have found in cities a fertile ground for growth, which, in turn, creates employment opportunities that stimulate the economic dynamo.

A prime example can be found in Copenhagen, a city lauded for its commitment to becoming carbon-neutral by 2025. This ambitious goal has led to a surge in green jobs, from cycling infrastructure projects to wind energy research, contributing an estimated growth in employment of about 15% in related sectors. Such green initiatives not only support job creation but also empower cities to become pioneers on the global stage, showcasing what can be achieved with ambitious policy frameworks.

Furthermore, sustainable urban planning reduces long-term economic costs associated with environmental degradation and resource overuse. Emphasizing energy efficiency alone can significantly cut costs for businesses and residents. Less money spent on energy means more money available to flow into local economies, spurring growth and improving the quality of life.

Economic resilience, particularly in the face of climate change, is another benefit that sustainable cities offer. By designing cities with resilience in mind—such as elevating structures, integrating natural flood defenses, or altering zoning laws—they shield themselves from the devastating financial impacts of natural disasters. A report by the Global Commission on the Economy and Climate highlighted that investing in resilience measures can yield trillions in avoided costs, not to mention the preservation of livelihoods and infrastructure.

Transportation is a critical area where sustainability and economics intersect, offering opportunities for major cost savings and revenue creation. Sustainable public transport systems, like the metro networks in Delhi or Seoul, reduce dependency on personal vehicles, cutting down fossil fuel use and lowering commuter costs. Moreover, reliable public transport is a significant draw for people and businesses alike, eager to avoid the congestion and pollution typical of car-centric urban areas.

Cities that embrace sustainable transport even see indirect economic benefits. Less congestion means faster, more reliable commutes, translating into productivity gains. Cleaner air invariably leads to less stressed, healthier populations, resulting in reduced healthcare costs and an increase in available workdays. An employee not forced to battle smog and gridlock is a happier, more efficient worker, after all.

Real estate markets in sustainable cities also demonstrate robust economic performance. Properties integrated with sustainable features—whether it be energy-efficient appliances, green roofs, or proximity to green spaces— are becoming increasingly attractive to buyers and renters. They typically command higher price points and rental yields, reflecting the growing value placed on sustainability by the market.

Moreover, cities that commit to sustainability attract legions of tourists eager to experience these eco-friendly marvels. Tourism, being a substantial economic contributor, benefits enormously from sustainable practices. Tourists are not just visiting; they're increasingly aware of their carbon footprint and are more drawn to destinations where they can experience lush parks, clean waterways, and eco-conscious hospitality. This added layer of visitor appeal translates directly into economic gain, fueling local businesses.

By supporting local ecosystems and biodiversity through sustainable practices such as urban farming and green corridors, cities can also tap into the economic potential of ecosystem services. These services provide benefits like pollination, stormwater regulation, and recreational opportunities, all of which have measurable economic value. Urban areas enriched with biodiverse environments offer vital respite for residents, enhance property values, and support local agriculture and fisheries.

Finally, sustainable cities are proving to be epicenters of social equity, a critical component of long-term economic stability. By ensuring equitable access to sustainable infrastructure and green spaces, cities foster inclusive growth where every segment of society benefits. Education and job training programs focused on green skills ensure that marginalized communities are not left behind, leveling the playing field and enriching the talent pool.

Sustainable cities are more than just an ecological imperative; they are engines of economic prosperity and resilience. By weaving sustainability into their fabric, cities can unlock growth, attract investment, and fortify themselves against future challenges. Sustainable practices are no longer peripheral or politically correct—they are central to thriving urban economies and the well-being of the millions who call cities their home. Embracing this model paves the way for a future where economic vitality and ecological balance are not only compatible but complementary.

2.4   Social and Health Implications

In the hustle and bustle of urban life, where concrete jungles stretch to the horizon, the subtle yet profound links between sustainability, social equity, and public health often go unnoticed. Yet, these connections are vital, weaving the tapestry of thriving, inclusive communities. Sustainability in cities is not merely an environmental or economic concern; it fundamentally redefines the social and health fabric, making urban spaces more equitable, healthier, and just.

Let's start with a fundamental premise: cities are crucibles of diversity. They bring together individuals from myriad cultural, socioeconomic, and linguistic backgrounds. However, this diversity can sometimes manifest disparities in access to resources, creating pockets of privilege next to areas of neglect. Here, sustainability initiatives shine, offering pathways to bridge these divides.

For instance, consider access to green spaces—a simple yet profound aspect of urban design that influences both social equity and public health. Studies have consistently shown that neighborhoods with accessible parks and recreation areas encourage physical activity, reduce stress, and improve mental health. Yet, inner-city residents, often from marginalized communities, may have limited access to such spaces. Sustainable urban planning that prioritizes creating and maintaining green areas throughout all neighborhoods ensures that these benefits are more equitably shared.

Furthermore, sustainable cities are designed to be inclusive, where infrastructure caters to individuals of all abilities. Low-carbon transport systems not only reduce emissions but also promote equity by providing affordable, reliable ways for people to access jobs, education, and healthcare. Cities like Amsterdam, with its intricate network of cycle paths, exemplify urban environments where transportation is both sustainable and socially inclusive.

Public health receives a substantial boost from sustainable practices. Cleaner air and water, reduced toxic emissions, and accessible green spaces translate directly into health benefits. Respiratory diseases, cardiovascular conditions, and mental health issues can be alleviated with thoughtful urban design. Consider the example of Berlin, which has implemented a range of air quality measures—from low-emission zones to extensive tree planting—resulting in measurable improvements in public health outcomes.

Another critical layer is the role of sustainable cities in fostering community resilience. In the face of climate change and other challenges, sustainable practices arm communities with the tools to withstand and recover from disruptions. When urban areas are designed with resilience in mind—incorporating flood defenses, community gardens, or solar energy installations—they build stronger social cohesion and self-reliance, enabling neighborhoods to thrive even under stress.

Educational opportunities also play a central role in the interplay between sustainability, social equity, and health. A focus on sustainability in education not only raises awareness about environmental impacts but empowers young people with the knowledge and skills to innovate and advocate for change. Cities with strong educational programs focused on sustainability ensure that all demographic groups are engaged in shaping a healthier and more equitable future.

Cities that embrace sustainability actively work to reduce energy poverty. Energy-efficient buildings and appliances, alongside renewable energy initiatives, lower utility costs for residents, particularly benefiting low-income families. By making energy more affordable, cities help alleviate financial stress, contributing to improved mental health and overall well-being.

Sustainability also fosters economic inclusion. As cities transition to greener economies, new job opportunities arise in emerging industries, like renewable energy, green construction, and sustainable transport.   By ensuring that skill development and access to these industries are inclusive, cities can significantly impact social mobility and economic equity.

Moreover, sustainable practices in urban agriculture and food systems enhance social equity and health by increasing food security.   Community gardens and urban farms, often located in underserved neighborhoods, provide fresh produce, reduce transportation emissions, and offer opportunities for education and community building.   Initiatives like Detroit's urban agriculture movement revitalizes not only landscapes but community engagement and cooperation.

The social dynamics of a sustainable city promote participation and empowerment.   In Barcelona, for instance, the "superblock" concept elevates citizen involvement, transforming streets into pedestrian-friendly zones. This approach encourages residents to partake in decision-making processes, fostering a shared sense of responsibility and belonging—a hallmark of both sustainability and social capital.

A deeper look at sustainability through a health lens reveals the importance of access to nature in urban settings. "Nature prescribing," a growing trend where healthcare providers recommend spending time in green spaces, illustrates the profound connection between environment and well-being. Cities rich with biodiversity and natural areas offer not just aesthetic pleasure but tangible health benefits.

The social and health implications of sustainable

cities are vast and interconnected. By promoting sustainability, urban areas can transcend traditional divisions, cultivating environments where every resident enjoys the fruits of ecological balance, economic opportunities, and good health. As cities march toward a sustainable future, they construct not only resilient infrastructures and economies but also vibrant, inclusive communities where social equity and public health thrive hand in hand.

2.5 Measuring Urban Sustainability

In the grand quest for sustainable urban development, measurement becomes both compass and map—a means not only to set a course but to chart progress along the way. Measuring urban sustainability is no simple feat; it encompasses a bewildering array of factors, each tying into the buzzing fabric of city life. Nonetheless, the tools and methodologies at our disposal are becoming ever more sophisticated, providing critical insights into how our cities perform and where there is room for improvement.

Urban sustainability measurement is akin to a symphony, where different instruments must harmonize to create a cohesive whole. Equitable growth, ecological health, and economic vitality all play essential roles. The challenge lies in capturing this nuance and complexity in tangible metrics. Here, sustainability indicators and assessments step in, functioning as the conductor's baton guiding the entire ensemble.

Historically, city planning focused predominantly on infrastructure and economic output, often sidelining environmental and social parameters. However, this has shifted with the acknowledgment that true urban prosperity is intrinsically linked to balanced sustainability. Developed over the second half of the 20th century, sophisticated frameworks now balance these domains, and tools like the United Nations' Sustainable Development Goals (SDGs) explicitly target urban sustainability, with goals dedicated to making cities inclusive, safe, resilient, and sustainable.

Let us consider one of the most comprehensive frameworks available: the Global City Indicator Facility (GCIF). This platform standardizes metrics across various dimensions—economic, environmental, social, and cultural—garnering data to compare cities on a global scale. It assesses 115 indicators, including access to public services, air quality, and social inclusivity, providing a robust profile through which cities can benchmark themselves against peers.

The Ecological Footprint is another pivotal measurement tool, translating humanity's consumption patterns into the area required to support them, allowing cities to identify their environmental load. Simply put, it measures how much nature we have and how much nature we use. A powerful visualization of this concept helps elucidate the contrast between a city's consumption and its biocapacity, urging a recalibration toward sustainability.

Yet metrics alone cannot capture the intangible aspects of urban life—happiness and satisfaction are equally critical components conveying quality of life. Thus, the Happy Planet Index makes its way into the sustainability measurement toolkit. By evaluating well-being alongside ecological efficiency and inequality, it provides an insightful balance often missing from traditional indicators. Cities like San Francisco, renowned for their livability and vibrant social structures, have benefited greatly from such approaches.

Importantly, technology has revolutionized how we collect and interpret urban sustainability data. Smart city initiatives now leverage the Internet of Things (IoT), GIS mapping, and Big Data analytics to provide real-time snapshots of urban dynamics. Barcelona's smart city strategy, for example, uses sensors throughout the city to monitor everything from air quality to energy use in real-time, reducing costs and enhancing functionality. Thanks to such innovations, cities swiftly adjust practices, ensuring sustainable outcomes are not just theoretical but actively managed.

Further, dashboards tailored to specific contexts, like the Doughnut Economy Model for sustainable development, offer a novel lens through which to view urban performance, highlighting gaps between actual and ideal conditions. This model juxtaposes social foundation pressures against ecological boundaries, urging cities to develop policies that keep them within a "safe and just space." Amsterdam—the first city to officially adopt this model—has designed urban policies to reflect both local and global sustainability targets, showcasing its adaptability to diverse socio-economic terrains.

Recognizing the imperative for more holistic approaches, many cities have adopted participatory methodologies for sustainability assessments, engaging local communities in data collection and decision making. Participatory GIS, for instance, enlists urban residents to map local resources and needs, ensuring sustainability initiatives reflect their lived experiences, not just top-down mandates.

While these systems are robust, challenges remain. Data quality and availability vary, complicating comparisons across different contexts. Metrics can become unwieldy or misinterpreted without clear communication. Moreover, there lingers an innate complexity in capturing the dynamic interactions of urban systems—efforts that can run afoul of reductionist tendencies.

Despite these hurdles, the trajectory is optimistic. Emerging cities like Kigali and Curitiba ambitiously push sustainability agendas, leveraging tailored metrics as guideposts for progress.   These benchmarking exercises not only guide their own development but serve as inspiration and blueprint for others aspiring to balance growth with ecological harmony.

Ultimately, measuring urban sustainability is a complex, but rewarding endeavor, crucial to fostering resilient, dynamic cities equipped to face contemporary challenges.   By building on past knowledge and embracing novel methodologies, cities of the future can continually strive toward becoming environments where planet and people prosper in concert. The tools we wield provide not just feedback but empowerment, guiding us ever further toward the sustainable urban ideal.

Chapter 3

Urban Planning and Design for Sustainability

This chapter discusses how urban planning and design are critical to achieving sustainability, focusing on principles like efficient land use, natural integration, and innovative architecture. It emphasizes creating compact, livable spaces that reduce ecological impact and the importance of community-driven planning processes. Through strategic design, cities can foster environments that support sustainable living, enhance quality of life, and maintain ecological integrity.

3.1 Principles of Sustainable Urban Design

Imagine a city that welcomes you with the serene hum of nature, seamlessly intertwined with bustling urban life. Streets brim with trees, offering shade and sweetness in the breeze, while parks extend invitations for spontaneous interaction with your neighbors. This vision isn't utopian fantasy; it's the ambition of sustainable urban design.

Sustainably designing urban spaces is akin to composing a symphony where every element—land, water, energy, and human activity—works in harmony. As with any sophisticated arrangement, this requires a foundational set of principles. Let's delve into these guiding precepts, weaving through historical context and contemporary applications to unfurl a tapestry of sustainable urbanism.

Density Done Right

Density in urban design initially brings to mind overcrowded streets and the jostling throng of humanity, but in sustainable contexts, it heralds a far more sophisticated concept—proximity. Sustainable designs cultivate compactness to reduce infrastructure strain, transportation costs, and ecological footprints, promoting walkability and vibrant public lives. Historically, cities like Barcelona adopted the Eixample Plan in the 19th century, orchestrating broad avenues and square blocks that allowed sunlight to bathe residential areas and residents to interconnect organically.

Taking a cue from this illustrious model, modern cities like Copenhagen have embraced density to drive sustainability. Here, bike-friendly infrastructure and pedestrian zones replace car dependency, showcasing how intelligent land use can curtail emissions and enhance life quality. Thus, density, recalibrated, becomes more than just packing people together; it's about bringing them closer to life's necessities in an eco-conscientious manner.

Harmony with Nature

On a more elemental note, integrating green spaces within urban landscapes establishes a symbiotic relationship between cities and nature. The idea here is not mere greenwashing but rather embracing nature as an indispensable facet of urban experience. Public parks, vertical gardens, and green roofs aren't just cosmetic; they breathe new life into concrete jungles, help manage stormwater, reduce the urban heat island effect, and elevate mental well-being.

Delve into the illustrious High Line in New York City, a relic from its storied past reimagined into a lush pedestrian promenade: an archetype of how we might re-envision neglected urban spaces. The result is not only a pulsating vein of biodiversity but a dynamic social corridor that nurtures community spirit and ecological mindfulness.

Resource Wisdom

At its heart, sustainability revolves around resource efficiency—utilizing what we have with prudence and foresight. From energy-efficient buildings harnessing solar power to rainwater harvesting systems capturing Earth's bounty, resource wisdom covers a spectrum of innovations. This principle extends to adaptive reuse of structures, turning the old into new marvels—echoing architect Carl Elefante's sentiment, "The greenest building is... one that is already built."

Examples abound, with Melbourne's Council House 2 setting a benchmark in green building standards by utilizing advanced ventilation systems and recycled materials. This notion of energy and resource stewardship fortifies urban resilience, reducing the environmental strain while fostering economic and social gains for future generations.

Inclusivity and Participation

While concrete and glass form a city's physical essence, its soul rests in its inhabitants. Sustainable urban design fundamentally hinges upon inclusivity—ensuring spaces are accessible and equitable. Participation invites community voices into the urban narrative,

sparking dialogue and co-creation. Community
gardens, for instance, proliferate in cities as venues for
cultivation and collaboration—a grassroots approach to
sustainability.

Take Curitiba, Brazil, where civic participation became
the cornerstone of its transformation into a paragon of
urban planning. Community engagement and social
equality guided development, resulting in an integrated
public transit system that reduced citywide inequality.
Their success illustrates another cardinal principle: a
city thrives when its residents don't just exist within it
but actively steward its growth.

Resilience Amid Change

Cities, like all complex systems, face constant flux—
be it climatic shifts, population surges, or economic
upheavals. The mark of a resilient urban framework lies
in its ability to absorb such shocks while maintaining
essential functions. Building adaptability into urban
design is akin to giving cities the gift of longevity.

Rotterdam's ingenious Water Squares convert public
spaces into flood management systems during storms, a
testament to resilient innovation. Such solutions make
clear that sustainability isn't a static goal but a dynamic
pursuit, requiring cities to anticipate and evolve with
the winds of change.

Cultural and Aesthetic Integration

Sustainable urban design isn't just functional; it's an art
form as well. Cities are cultural expressions, and sustainability isn't at odds with beauty. From vernacular architecture embracing local materials and cultures to public
art installations that awaken civic pride, aesthetics play
a critical role in urban resilience and identity.

The delights of cities like Kyoto reside in their ability

to meld the architecture of tradition with modern ingenuity—crafting spaces where past and present coexist in harmony. These culturally rich environments contribute distinct flavors to urban life, reinforcing that sustainability is as much a celebration of heritage as a call to future possibilities.

Bridging Now and Future

Sustainable urban design is a manifesto for the present and a promise for the future. By entwining these core principles, cities can transform into havens of ecological balance, human prosperity, and enduring resilience. Such cities emerge as living ecosystems, nurturing our coexistence with the planet and each other.

Ultimately, the canvas of urban possibility is limitless. In imagining—and materializing—cities that pulse with sustainability, we script stories of hope, aspiration, and shared destiny. This symphony of design and innovation invites us all to compose cities where future generations will not only live but thrive. The invitation is open—to create, to sustain, and to dream of spaces where life blooms in all its holistic splendor.

3.2 Compact and Efficient Land Use

Picture a city that makes the most of every inch of its landscape, where human endeavor coexists harmoniously with the natural world, and where the day's necessities lie just a short distance away. This vision reflects the core idea behind compact and efficient land use—a cornerstone of sustainable urban design.

Unlike sprawling urban developments that consume land with reckless abandon, efficient land use springs from the philosophy of doing more with less. The crux of this approach lies in creating vibrant, multifunctional spaces that celebrate proximity and accessibility, ultimately reducing our ecological footprint. This section will reveal the magic of space optimization, drawing on historical legacies and modern innovations to paint a picture of urban efficiency.

The Value of Compactness

Consider the grandeur of ancient Rome, where the city's compact layout facilitated not only the swift movement of legions but also the flourishing of commerce and culture. Fast forward to today, and the globe's most enduring cities continue to leverage this principle by maintaining high population densities coupled with efficient land use. The magic of compactness lies in its ability to reduce the need for extensive infrastructure and transportation while preserving the land for future generations.

Compact urban forms spark economic vibrancy and foster human connections. They enable economies of scale, making public transport viable and sustainable. Cities like Singapore excel by embracing compactness, showcasing how efficient planning can support both economic dynamism and an enviable quality of life, despite spatial limitations.

Mixing It Up: The Art of Mixed-Use Development

In the world of harmonious urban spaces, single-use zoning is akin to playing a one-note tune. Mixed-use development, by contrast, orchestrates a symphony, where residential, commercial, and recreational areas coexist and complement one another. This arrangement not only reduces the need for long commutes but also invigorates local economies and promotes active, pedestrian-friendly environments.

Think of Melbourne's Docklands, a swath of formerly industrial landscape reimagined into a thriving area bustling with life around the clock. Restaurants, offices, apartments, and leisure spaces mingle, crafting a vibrant urban ecosystem. By combining multiple uses within a single area, cities breathe life into every square meter, translating efficiency into experience.

The Tale of Transit-Oriented Development

In many modern cities, the car demands vast expanses of land, inhibiting connectivity and exacerbating congestion. Transit-oriented development (TOD) presents a counter-narrative: one that places public transportation at the heart of urban planning. It advocates for high-density development around transit nodes, maximizing accessibility and minimizing reliance on private vehicles.

Tokyo emerges as a shining beacon of TOD success. Enveloped by an elaborate transit system, the city's districts are seamlessly interconnected, allowing the rapid movement of millions without the environmental toll exacted by car reliance. Through strategic planning, cities orchestrate land use around transport hubs, weaving networks of efficiency and reducing carbon footprints.

Breathing Room: Public Spaces in Compact Cities

Efficient does not equate to barren. In compact cities, public spaces serve as the lungs of urban landscapes, offering much-needed areas of relief and social interaction. These spaces don't just provide aesthetic or recreational value; they contribute to the ecological well-being and adaptability of cities, offering stormwater management, biodiversity habitats, and corridors for circulation.

Consider the transformative potential evidenced by Medellín, Colombia. Once notorious for its urban challenges, Medellín revitalized its neighborhoods by integrating public spaces such as parks and trails,

connected by metro and cable lift systems. The result
is a city that thrives both socially and environmentally,
unlocking new opportunities for civic engagement and
ecological restoration.

Languages of Land: Adaptive Reuse and Repurposing

With sustainability in mind, cities can speak the
languages of their land by adapting and repurposing
existing structures. Turning an unused warehouse into
a community center or a derelict factory space into
a bustling arts hub can breathe new life into an area,
preserving its history while adapting to contemporary
needs.

The success of Seattle's Amazon Spheres illustrates this
principle. By repurposing urban space, the city created
an innovative, verdant work environment that stands as
a testament to innovative land use. Such projects deliver
economic and environmental returns while conserving
resources and maintaining cultural fabric.

The Green Dividend: Agriculture in Urban Land Use

For many urban areas, the allure of self-sufficiency
is captured by bringing agriculture within city limits.
Urban agriculture—rooftop gardens, community plots,
and vertical farming—opens new dialogues about food
security and ecological balance. Copenhagen, with its
Byhaven 2200 community garden in Nørrebro, provides
a model for such initiatives, offering both recreational
space and food production within a dense urban setting.

Urban agriculture enhances land efficiency, fostering
a closer relationship between residents and their food
sources while reducing food miles and carbon emissions.
It transforms cities into self-sustaining environments
where nature and development coalesce harmoniously.

The Path Forward

The narrative of compact and efficient land use offers cities abundant opportunities to embrace sustainability while fostering economic resilience and societal well-being. Compactness, mixed-use development, public spaces, and innovative repurposing create urban systems that perform gracefully under the weight of modern challenges.

In forging the path forward, cities face the dual quests of innovation and preservation. They must honor historical roots while accommodating growing populations and advancing technological triumphs. In achieving this balance, urban landscapes become spaces of possibility where sustainable living, economic vitality, and social harmony thrive in unison.

As we navigate the evolving discourse on sustainable urbanism, we must remember that every city holds the potential for transformation. Our task is to harness this potential through smart land use strategies that cultivate cities for people and their planet—a journey toward crafting spaces where stories unfold, communities blossom, and futures are forged, all within the vibrant confines of compact cityscapes.

3.3 Integrating Nature into Urban Spaces

Envision a city where birdsong competes with morning traffic and verdant corridors connect urbanites to their wild roots. Integrating nature into urban spaces not only crafts delightful aesthetics but serves as a vital strategy for sustainability, providing ecological, economic, and societal benefits. The success of this integration hinges on thoughtful planning and creative reuse of existing environments. Herein lies the story of cities becoming vibrant habitats for both humanity and nature.

The Nature of Cities: A Historical Primer

The notion of integrating natural elements into cityscapes is hardly novel. In fact, its roots dig deep into human consciousness, stretching back to early civilizations.   Consider medieval European towns, where city walls fringed with pastoral landscapes nurtured a symbiotic relationship between human settlements and nature. Fast forward to the 19th century, and Frederick Law Olmsted's pioneering vision manifested in grand urban green spaces like New York City's Central Park—a testament to nature's healing power amidst the industrial revolution's turmoil.

Today's challenge lies in scaling these principles to meet the demands of a burgeoning urban populace. With half the world's population residing in cities, the quest to harmonize urbanity with nature remains urgent.

Green Arteries: The Network of Natural Corridors

Modern urban planners reshape cities by introducing green corridors—linear parks that wend through the cityscape, stitching together neighborhoods and ecosystems alike.   These green arteries do more than connect—they serve as critical wildlife pathways, facilitating species movement and promoting biodiversity within urban areas.

London's extensive network of Greenways exemplifies this approach, providing recreational trails alongside habitats for flora and fauna.   By transforming underutilized lands into verdant passageways, cities can create breathing frameworks that sustain both wildlife and wellness.

Rooftop Gardens: The New Urban Canopy

Where terrestrial space is constrained, urban biodiversity can thrive atop rooftops. Turning gray roofs into lush ecosystems not only enhances aesthetics but also improves air quality, combats the urban heat island effect, and aids energy conservation.

Toronto's Green Roof Bylaw mandates green roofing on new construction, blending civic regulation with ecological wisdom. These elevated gardens offer tranquil hideaways amid the urban hustle, a retreat just one flight away, fostering mental and physical rejuvenation by reconnecting residents with nature above their busy streets.

Nature's Envelope: Buildings Embrace Biodiversity

Biophilic design embraces nature as intrinsic to our living environments, threading elements like natural light, vegetation, and water throughout architectural spaces. By embedding nature into the fabric of buildings, urban areas become sanctuaries of inclusion for human and non-human life.

Consider the Bosco Verticale in Milan, a vertical forest that populates apartment balconies with thousands of trees and shrubs. This innovative design serves as both residence and mini ecosystem, blending urban living with natural symphony, while reducing air pollutants and fostering wildlife habitat.

Community Gardens: Sowing Seeds in Concrete

Community green spaces are powerful instruments for urban renewal, forging social bonds while cultivating local produce. They transform empty lots into fertile ground, acting as neighborhood anchors that yield bountiful returns—economic, ecological, and social.

Berlin's Prinzessinnengärten exemplifies a movement towards collective urban agriculture, where residents reclaim sterile spaces for organic cultivation. Such initiatives teach environmental stewardship, offer community engagement, and connect people over the shared harvest. They invite urbanites to play an active role in shaping their environment, turning concrete trays into cornucopias.

Waterscapes: Reshaping Urban Waterways

Rivers, lakes, and shores carve cities with their fluid touch. Integrating these aquatic resources within urban designs revives natural lifelines, affording ecological sanctuaries amidst bustling city life.

Cheonggyecheon Stream in Seoul paints a striking example: once buried under roadways, this revitalized urban stream now runs through the heart of the city, offering an untamed escape for both wildlife and pedestrians. The stream stands as a beacon of ecological reclamation, fostering diverse life while cooling city air and providing recreation.

Urban Tree Canopies: Shade Above, Paths Below

Trees, the stalwarts of natural integration, offer myriad benefits to city dwellers. Urban tree canopies address air quality, climate regulation, and mental well-being while reducing noise pollution. Giant umbrellas of green, they shelter pedestrians and wildlife alike, transforming streets into cooled sanctuaries.

Singapore's ambitious City in Nature initiative outlines a commitment to green cover, envisioning greenery lining every street and trail. These arboreal landmarks stand as testaments to the city's innovative resilience—urban form meets natural function.

The Green Promise

Integrating nature into urban spaces is not merely an

aspiration; it is an imperative endeavor aligned with sustainable futures. By weaving nature into the urban mosaic, cities can serve as both habitats and hearths, with paths of progress twinned by expanses of green.

These landscapes encapsulate possibilities where humanity and nature coexist in harmony—the art of thriving in tandem. Our cities, as living organisms, perpetually evolve, adopting these green principles to redefine futures rooted in equilibrium. Embrace the ethos of urban natural integration, and watch as cities bloom into habitats of collective growth and spirited expression.

3.4 Innovative Architectural Approaches

A city's skyline is its markup—a testament to how it utilizes space, energy, and imagination. In the relentless pursuit of sustainability, architecture becomes a keystone, where innovative designs can transform urban landscapes. Imagine buildings as living entities, harmonizing with their environment to preserve resources and enhance our quality of life. This section delves into how architectural ingenuity serves as an agent of sustainable urban evolution.

The Legacy of Sustainable Design

The concept of sustainable architecture isn't a modern marvel but a rediscovery of ancient wisdom. Early builders in arid regions relied on passive techniques for cooling and ventilation, such as thick walls and courtyards that regulated temperature. These practices laid the groundwork for contemporary sustainable design, showcasing a legacy of environmental symbiosis that's more relevant today than ever.

In the modern age, sustainable architecture evolved dramatically with the advent of the green building movement. Propelled by environmental awareness and technological advances, this movement embraces innovative materials and techniques to reduce the ecological footprint of buildings significantly.

Biomimicry: Nature-Inspired Design

Nature, in all its efficiency, provides an extensive catalogue of lessons for sustainable architecture. Biomimicry draws directly from this inspiration, imitating natural processes to enhance building performance. Structures that mimic the self-cooling properties of termite mounds or the water-collecting capabilities of beetles offer startling innovations in design.

Harare's Eastgate Centre epitomizes biomimetic architecture. Its design, inspired by the ventilation system of a termite mound, acts without conventional air conditioning, maintaining a more comfortable climate indoors and reducing energy consumption drastically.

The Rise of Smart Materials

Smart materials represent a quantum leap in architectural innovation, bringing a dynamic ability to respond to environmental stimuli. These materials alter their properties—think windows that change tint in response to light, or paint that repairs itself—tailoring building skins to the immediate weather conditions.

Take, for example, the Milan Expo's Italian Pavilion, which utilized photocatalytic concrete. This material not only absorbs pollution but also reduces harmful substances in the air, showcasing an intelligent blend of form and function that benefits urban ecosystems.

Net-Zero Buildings: Sustainability by the Numbers

Stepping into the realm of net-zero, buildings become powerhouses of efficiency—producing as much energy as they consume, or even contributing excess back to the grid. Net-zero initiatives hinge on a trifecta of energy conservation, renewable energy use, and efficiency maximization.

The Bullitt Center in Seattle flaunts its net-zero credentials, boasting solar panels, composting toilets, and rainwater recycling systems. As one of the world's greenest commercial buildings, it exemplifies how integrating high-performance systems into design holds the key to sustainability.

Vertical Farms: Rethinking Agriculture

Amid the concrete expanses of urban centers, vertical farms fertilize the link between architecture and agriculture. They repurpose vertical spaces to grow produce, maximizing yield per square foot and reducing the carbon footprint associated with traditional farming.

Tokyo's Pasona Urban Farm underscores the viability of this approach. Integrating lush greenery within office spaces, the farm harvests vegetables and fish, creating a self-sustaining ecosystem and offering employees fresher air and food. This venture seamlessly blends agricultural ingenuity with urban design, rejuvenating the concept of food security.

Tiny Houses: A Minimally Imposing Footprint

The tiny house movement postulates that less is more—offering an alternative lifestyle that values minimalism and energy efficiency over excess. These small structures utilize space-efficient layouts and innovative materials to deliver sustainable living to urbanites without compromise.

Architects have fueled this trend with homes like those

in the Tumbleweed community in Sonoma, which leverage reclaimed materials and off-grid systems to achieve
their goals. Tiny homes challenge conventional notions
of design and encourage a paradigm shift towards minimal impact.

Adaptive Reuse: Breathing New Life into the Old

Architecture isn't always about building anew. Adaptive
reuse transforms existing structures into contemporary
marvels, conserving embodied energy and cultural heritage. By retaining foundational elements, this practice
offers considerable savings in resources and energy.

Boston's Innovation and Design Building, once a ship-
ping warehouse, is now a hub for creativity and technology after thoughtful renovations. It underscores adaptive reuse's potential to infuse life, character, and economic activity into aging architecture, championing sustainability without sacrificing style.

The Future of Green Design

As cities endeavor to achieve sustainable futures,
architecture remains at the helm of this trajectory. The
commitment to pioneering designs that fuse form and
function, utility and beauty, results in cities that inspire
progress without sacrificing ecological integrity.

Through embracing innovative techniques and
materials, we shape urban habitats where sustainability
is intrinsic rather than an addendum. In crafting these
luminous legacies of ingenuity, cities offer narratives of
necessity transformed into art—the pinnacle of harmony
between people and planet. From metamorphic facades
to energy-generating edifices, sustainable architecture
elevates our imagination and expectation, painting
blueprints of cities where coexistence is not only an
ambition but a reality.

3.5 Community-Driven Planning

Imagine a city where the voices of its inhabitants reverberate through every street, park, and building—a place sculpted by the needs and dreams of those who call it home. Welcome to the realm of community-driven planning, where the heartbeats of urban spaces pulse in harmony with their residents' aspirations. This approach champions inclusive development, ensuring that the blueprint of sustainability reflects the collective wisdom and creativity of its community.

The Roots of Inclusive Planning

Before diving into the living tapestry of community-driven planning, we must acknowledge its roots. Throughout history, many planning efforts neglected grassroots participation, resulting in cities that often felt imposing and alienating to residents. Post-World War II urban renewal projects, particularly in the United States, displaced entire communities in favor of wide expressways and monolithic complexes, leading to social fragmentation and civic disengagement.

In response, a paradigm shift emerged. People began to reclaim their voices, demanding a say in the landscapes they inhabited. The 1960s and 1970s saw the rise of participatory planning—a movement invigorated by civic engagement and social activism. This new wave fostered transparency and trust, laying the foundation for modern community-driven endeavors.

Participation: The Soul of Sustainable Cities

Participation is the lifeblood of community-driven planning, infusing projects with authenticity and durability. When individuals contribute to urban development, they bring diverse perspectives and innovative solutions that might otherwise be overlooked.

Through workshops, charrettes, and public meetings, community members transform from passive recipients to proactive partners in city planning.

Take the example of Porto Alegre, Brazil, a beacon of participatory budgeting. Each year, citizens engage in dialogue about local priorities, directly influencing the allocation of municipal funds. This not only empowers residents but also fosters accountability and responsiveness, nurturing trust and civic pride.

The Wisdom of Crowds: Unleashing Collective Intelligence

Community-driven planning taps into the collective intelligence of its populace, sparking novel ideas and adaptive solutions. By gathering insights from the people who intimately understand their environment, cities can craft spaces that resonate with the lived experiences of their inhabitants.

Consider the High Line in New York City, a masterpiece of iterative design. Initially an obsolete rail line, the High Line's transformation into a linear park was propelled by community vision. Through grassroots efforts and civic collaboration, residents reimagined a blighted infrastructure into a vibrant urban oasis—a testament to communal creativity.

Equity and Justice: Planning with Purpose

In many urban landscapes, the quest for sustainability is intertwined with the pursuit of social justice. Community-driven planning places equity at the forefront, ensuring marginalized voices are amplified and considered in decision-making. This approach helps dismantle systemic barriers, promoting inclusivity and fairness.

Take Boston's Dudley Street Neighborhood Initiative—a

hallmark of equitable development. Faced with disinvestment and neglect, residents banded together to reclaim their neighborhood, fostering affordable housing, green spaces, and small business growth. The initiative illustrates how community agency can catalyze transformation, balancing economic development with environmental stewardship.

Tech Connections: The Digital Age of Planning

Incorporating technology into community-driven planning broadens participation and enhances transparency. Digital platforms and social media invite citizens into virtual forums, enabling real-time feedback and collaborative design. Such tools cultivate an open dialogue, bridging gaps between planners and residents.

Ithaca, New York, exemplifies this digital engagement through its crowdsourced GIS mapping initiatives, empowering residents to propose and visualize urban improvements. The result is a dynamic exchange where ideas flourish, integrating technology into the urban lexicon of collaboration.

Resilience Through Shared Stewardship

Community-driven planning equips cities to adapt in a rapidly changing world. Resilient urban environments emerge not only from sustainable design but also from shared stewardship and local knowledge. By fostering strong community bonds and ownership, cities become more resilient to socioeconomic and environmental shifts.

Imagine the response in Christchurch, New Zealand, following devastating earthquakes. The city's regeneration plans took root in community dialogue, ensuring that reconstruction met both practical needs and emotional well-being. This inclusivity catalyzed resilience, demonstrating that committed community involvement strengthens adaptability.

The Path Forward: Communities as Co-Creators

The essence of community-driven planning is co-creation—crafting urban solutions that are as dynamic and diverse as the communities they serve. By placing people at the heart of development, cities thrive as living mosaics that reflect the kaleidoscope of human experience.

Ultimately, the path forward for urban planners is to embrace partnership with communities, weaving the social fabric into each phase of development. By listening, engaging, and acting alongside residents, cities unlock their potential to become resilient, inclusive locales where everyone feels a sense of belonging.

Through collective vision and relentless dedication, community-driven planning cultivates urban futures forged by all, for all.

Chapter 4

Transportation and Mobility in the Future City

This chapter examines sustainable transportation solutions addressing current urban mobility challenges through efficient, eco-friendly models and innovations. It underscores the significance of public transit, emerging technologies like electric vehicles, and designing pedestrian-friendly environments. The focus is on developing integrated mobility systems that reduce congestion, minimize environmental impact, and improve accessibility, supporting the transition towards sustainable, livable urban spaces of the future.

4.1 Current Challenges in Urban Mobility

As bustling metropolises grow, they bear witness to the chaos of their own expansion. Urban mobility, once the bearer of progress and freedom, now finds itself tangled in the throes of modern-day challenges. Very much like a juggler with too many balls in the air, cities worldwide wrestle with issues that demand innovative, sustainable solutions. Understanding these challenges sets the stage for imagining the transportation systems of the future—

a future that not only pursues efficiency but also cherishes sustainability.

One of the most conspicuous challenges is the ever-present traffic congestion.   City streets, awash with vehicles, morph into vast parking lots during peak hours, stalling productivity and fraying patience.   The resulting economic costs are staggering, not to mention the personal time wasted while idling in bumper-to-bumper traffic. In Los Angeles, for example, commuters spend an average of 119 hours annually in congestion, underscoring the need for immediate intervention.

Even as congestion chokes our streets, air quality suffers profoundly.   Internal combustion engines, spewing pollutants, color the urban skies a dingy gray.   This pollution poses grave health risks, contributing to conditions such as asthma and heart disease.   The increase in particulate matter particularly affects urban residents, who often face a double burden when these harmful emissions intersect with other industrial pollutants.   With an estimated nine out of ten people breathing air that exceeds World Health Organization guidelines, the necessity for clean air becomes inescapable.

Embedded within the tangled web of urban transportation issues is the persistent inequality of access.   In sprawling cities, the lack of reliable transportation options can isolate communities, impeding access to employment, healthcare, and education.   The stark reality is that while some neighborhoods enjoy extensive public transit networks, others languish in transport deserts, creating an uneven patchwork of accessibility.   This disparity not only dictates where residents can work and live but also entrenches existing socio-economic divides.

Moreover, urban transportation systems are inextricably

linked to the consumption of finite resources. The overwhelming reliance on fossil fuels propels the depletion of these resources, fueling further environmental degradation. This dependency is a double-edged sword: the more we consume, the more we contribute to climate change, whose impacts—rising sea levels, extreme weather events—present additional challenges for cities worldwide.

To further complicate matters, the existing infrastructure in many cities is aging and inadequate to meet current demands, let alone future needs. Roads, bridges, and public transit systems creak under the strain of growing populations and vehicular loads. Maintenance and upgrading become monumental tasks, as cities struggle with funding and logistical hurdles. Urban areas find themselves at a crossroads, caught between pressing needs and finite budgets.

Amidst these logistical quagmires lies a human element, deeply intertwined with psychology and behavior. Habitual reliance on personal vehicles is a significant barrier to change. Car culture, deeply ingrained in the psyche of many societies, has built a formidable resistance to adopting more sustainable commuting practices. The convenience and perceived autonomy of personal cars often outweigh the drawbacks, with many unwilling to embrace public or shared transportation due to concerns about reliability, convenience, and comfort.

The digital age introduces yet another layer of complexity. The rise of rideshare services and home delivery logistics has, paradoxically, contributed to congestion, with app-driven vehicles perpetually on the move. While these technologies offer unprecedented convenience, they also exacerbate existing challenges, leading urban planners to reconsider traffic patterns and road usage.

In light of these intertwined challenges, the call for sustainable solutions is loud and clear. To transform from gridlock to greenways, cities must prioritize an integrated approach that marries technology with thoughtful planning. This entails not just addressing the symptoms but tackling the root causes with comprehensive policies. Enhancing public transit networks, incentivizing non-motorized transportation, and embracing smart technologies all form pieces of the puzzle.

Perhaps one path forward is reimagining the urban landscape itself, welcoming mixed-land use development that blends residential, commercial, and recreational spaces to reduce the need for long commutes. This strategy fosters environments where walking and biking are practical and desirable options, not mere afterthoughts.

Moreover, cities stand at the cusp of a renewable revolution. By leveraging renewable energy sources such as solar and wind, urban transport systems can significantly reduce their carbon footprints. Investment in electric and hydrogen-powered vehicles presents a viable solution, as does the creation of comprehensive networks of electric vehicle charging stations, encouraging a shift away from fossil fuels.

Ultimately, solving urban mobility challenges requires a collective commitment to responsive governance and community engagement. As cities implement change, they must also communicate its benefits, engendering public trust and cooperation. Success hinges on the participation of all stakeholders—from policymakers and businesses to individual citizens—each contributing to the harmonious symphony of a future city where mobility is as green as it is seamless.

So, as the modern-day urban juggler deftly balances these multifaceted challenges, it becomes evident that sustainable solutions are not mere alternatives but imperatives. A holistic, forward-thinking approach to urban mobility will pave the path to cities that are not only dynamic and efficient but ultimately resilient and sustainable.

4.2 Sustainable Transportation Models

If the cacophony of urban vehicular chaos were to have a sweet antidote, it would undoubtedly be the harmonious melody of sustainable transportation models. These counterpoints to traditional, car-reliant systems strive to redefine mobility not just by boosting efficiency and eco-friendliness, but by crafting a vision of cities where moving from point A to B doesn't come at the expense of the environment or our sanity.

To begin our exploration, it's crucial to acknowledge that at the heart of sustainable transportation lies the concept of integration—an ode to harmony between diverse modes of transport. Integration is achieved through systemic connectivity between various forms of mobility, ensuring a seamless experience for users who alternately hop on a bus, glide on a tram, or pedal a bike, depending on the task at hand. A prime exemplar of this model is Switzerland's public transit system, which stitches trains, trams, buses, and ferries into a comprehensive network. This tapestry of transportation means that over 80% of Swiss citizens have access to public transit within a mere kilometer of their homes, dramatically reducing the nation's dependence on cars.

The growth of bike-sharing programs globally

highlights another sustainable model.   These systems offer the simplicity and convenience of bicycle access without the binds of ownership.   Paris' Vélib', one of the earliest large-scale examples, set a gold standard by peppering the city with thousands of bikes readily available at docking stations.   More than a mere exercise in logistics, bike-sharing programs promote a culture of cycling, reshaping urban habits and reducing pollution in the bargain.

A contemporary companion to bike-sharing is the concept of car-sharing, fueled by the rise of companies like Zipcar and other community-based initiatives. Car-sharing platforms subscribe to the less-is-more philosophy. By providing short-term access to vehicles, these programs argue that fewer cars on the road can satisfy the same level of demand—emphasizing the utility of cars without necessitating ownership.   The success of these models suggests that the future may hold more parking spaces that languish empty.

Environmental   efficiency   coupled   with   public engagement lays at the core of Bus Rapid Transit (BRT) systems.   BRTs strive to marry the benefits of traditional bus travel with the speed and efficiency of rail transit.   By allocating dedicated lanes, optimizing boarding processes,   and   offering   frequent,   direct routes, BRTs reduce travel time and improve reliability. Curitiba, Brazil, introduced one of the earliest BRT systems in the 1970s, effectively transforming the city's traffic while highlighting public transport's potential as a driver of urban equity and sustainability.

Perhaps we might consider the allure of the electrified vehicle—both literal and figurative powerhouses of change. Electric vehicles (EVs), replete with advantages like zero tailpipe emissions and minimized noise pollution, are pivotal in the contemporary dialogue around sustainability. Cities such as Oslo have carved paths for these silent vehicles to whisper through the cityscape, facilitated by policy incentives, tax exemptions, and extensive charging networks. EVs are steadily migrating from the pages of science fiction to the streets we traverse daily, challenging us to reconsider energy's role in mobility.

Yet, innovation need not be confined to terrestrial transport. Navigating today's waterways offers its own canvas for sustainable transition. Return to Amsterdam and its canal delight, where electric boats offer tours of the city's iconic waterways without churning pollution into the sky. Reimagining urban waterways as routes for cargo and commuting heralds a return to traditional transport roots, albeit with a thoroughly modern twist.

Technarchies—urban design thinking in transportation— embody a holistic approach that encompasses not only mechanical efficiency but environmental and human well-being. Concepts such as Transit-Oriented Development (TOD) foreground the utility of connecting community needs to the transit network. This approach advocates for building dense, mixed-use communities designed around transit hubs to enhance mobility while promoting vibrant, walkable neighborhoods. Exempli gratia, Vancouver's Olympic Village is a beacon of TOD success, masterfully blending residential amenities with easy access to public transportation.

The digital heartbeat of the urban grid can be felt in Smart Mobility solutions which leverage cutting-edge technology to streamline movements through the cityscape. This comprehensive framework comprises tools such as real-time data systems, smart infrastructure, and algorithmic planning to mitigate congestion and optimize routing. These innovations extend a technological olive branch to nature by achieving operational efficiencies and reducing emissions.   Examples in Singapore and Helsinki showcase the fruits of smart transport, with data-driven platforms refining everything from traffic light patterns to dynamic toll pricing.

Adopting these models signals a paradigm shift: a chance to reframe transportation not as an independent actor but as part of an interconnected urban ecosystem. In essence, sustainable transportation models embody the mantra "think globally, act locally." As cities adopt these blueprints for mobility, they become crucibles for localized solutions capable of refinement and expansion.

Sustainable transportation models challenge us to critically reexamine the symbiotic relationship between people, place, and progression. As urbanization mounts an unrelenting march forward, visions of harmonious movement remind us that the momentum towards a better future rests not just on new technologies, but on the shoulders of collective willpower—a willpower that transcends mere transportation, reaching into the heart of human possibility.

4.3   Role of Public Transit

In the relentless hustle and bustle that defines urban life, public transit emerges as both an ancient art and an evolving science—a vital cog in the machinery that keeps cities vibrant and breathable. Like the circulatory system in a body, public transit networks tirelessly shuttle hordes of commuters, ensuring that the pulse of the city remains steady and strong. As cities burgeon and pressures mount, the role of public transportation in mitigating congestion and pollution becomes even more indispensable.

Let us first step back in time to appreciate the genesis of public transport. In the early 19th century, London's horse-drawn omnibus and New York's streetcars epitomized urban planning marvels, offering collective transportation solutions that lavished accessibility on residents. They sowed the seeds for today's intricate transport networks, evolving through the steam-powered locomotives of the Industrial Revolution to the electric streetcars of the early 20th century. This evolution bore witness to public transit's underlying promise: to mollify the chaos of rapid urbanization.

Fast-forward to the present day, and public transit systems have become essential civil infrastructure. Urban congestion—a menace plaguing cities worldwide—is public enemy number one, devouring time and fuel while spewing pollutants. The humble bus and train are poised as knights in shining armor, armed with the capacity to ferry thousands across urban landscapes in an efficient manner. The New York City subway system, for instance, serves four million passengers each weekday with relative ease, obviating the need for countless individual car journeys that would otherwise clog the city's arteries.

Moreover, the environmental dividends offered by public transit are hard to overstate. By luring potential car users onto buses and trains, cities can significantly cut down on emissions per capita. Consider the tram networks of Melbourne and Geneva, where electrically powered streetcars cruise seamlessly through cities, operated by energy sources increasingly leaning toward renewables. The switch from private car use to public transit, when executed on a large scale, echoes the profound reduction of carbon footprints, akin to a welcome breeze dispelling the urban smog.

Public transit's value transcends mere efficiency and environmental stewardship. It serves as an essential equalizer, democratizing mobility and fostering social equity. Accessible and affordable public transit networks enable all city dwellers, regardless of economic status, to partake in the urban experience. This is particularly evident in cities like Hong Kong, where the octopus card system facilitates both ease of movement and an egalitarian approach to urban exploration, shrinking distances not by kilometers but through shared access.

Technology, the relentless adapter, continues to infuse new life into this old framework. The rise of Transit Apps, integrated with user-friendly interfaces, grants commuters real-time data on routes and schedules, rendering the wait for a late bus a rarity. In North European cities such as Stockholm, public transit systems have been wedded to digital technology, where mobile apps keep passengers well-informed, and contactless payments expedite access. Technology is the bridge connecting citizens to efficiency and improving the transit experience, transforming what were once significant barriers into mere stepping stones.

Nevertheless, the challenges within public transit systems remain daunting. Infrastructure upkeep demands constant investment, with aging fleets and tracks calling for attention and investment. Political will, often mired in red tape and competing priorities, holds the power to either hinder or catalyze the transit evolution. Financing solutions, such as public-private partnerships, emerge as tools for innovation and expansion, unlocking potential collaborations that can renew sagging systems and accommodate soaring future demands.

Cities like Seoul and Singapore illustrate how strategic planning, coupled with a vision for the future, can enhance public transit to new heights. In Seoul, heavy rail lines supplemented by a vast network of buses create an interwoven fabric of connectivity, proving that meticulous planning offers not just logistical efficiency but an environmental boon. Successes in one city breed blueprints for others, lighting the path toward networks that effectively accommodate growing populations while curtailing emissions.

Public transit embodies more than a solution to congestion and pollution; it reflects a city's soul. It champions the idea that cities can be spaces of communal sharing rather than individual division. Public transportation systems, when robustly designed and equitably executed, knit the varied tapestry of urban life, enhancing quality of life while slimming environmental footprints. In this ever-spinning world, where urban centers appear like bustling ecosystems, public transit emerges as a guardian—a stabilizer churning the waters of change into avenues of hope. Its evolution is not just vital for the cities of today but indispensable for those of tomorrow.

Thus, as urban landscapes evolve, public transit will remain a pillar of resilience, a testament to human adeptness in crafting systems of connection. The future sees public transit not as a solution en route but a destination where the paths of sustainability, efficiency, and equity converge. As much as steel and concrete define modern cities, so too will the fluent movement of people within them define our success in forging a sustainable urban future.

4.4   Emerging Technologies in Mobility

In an age where smartphone apps can summon a car at the tap of a screen and electric vehicles hum like futuristic chariots along our streets, the roadmap of mobility is being redrawn by emerging technologies. Urban landscapes are poised on the brink of transformation, spurred by innovations that are not just enhancing how we move, but redefining our relationship with movement itself. As these technologies intertwine with our daily commutes, they promise to shift mobility from a tale of congestion and pollution to one of coherence and sustainability.

To chart this brave new world, we must look back to the incubation of one of its most heralded harbingers: the electric vehicle (EV). Emerging from a lineage of 19th-century experimentation, EVs have seen a tumultuous evolution—ranging from the electric buggies of the early 1900s to their eclipse by gasoline engines during the subsequent decades. Fast forward to the 21st century, and a renaissance is underway, driven by mounting environmental awareness and staggering advances in battery technology.

Today, electric vehicles are gaining traction in both policy circles and consumer garages. At the heart of this resurgence lies the lithium-ion battery, a powerhouse that catapulted EVs beyond early limitations of range and charging time. As charging infrastructure burgeons, cities like Oslo have showcased what electrification can achieve—proving that when public enthusiasm meets regulatory support, the resulting spark ignites transformative change.

Yet, in the multifaceted tapestry of modern mobility, electric engines represent just one thread. Autonomous transport strides into reality with vehicles that inch ever closer to independent navigation. The promise of self-driving cars conjures images of streamlined traffic, fewer accidents, and a world where drivers are free to muse over novels, meals, or morning rhythms instead of steering wheels.

However, this technological marvel is not without its hurdles. Machine learning algorithms and AI, the brains behind autonomy, continue to evolve, refining the nuances required to safely interact with unpredictable city streets. High-profile players such as Waymo and Tesla lead the charge, but the ultimate aspiration—fully autonomous level five vehicles—remains an exhilarating yet elusive goal. Moreover, questions loom large around cybersecurity, ethical decision-making, and the social repercussions of widespread adoption. These considerations remind us that while the vehicle may drive itself, society still holds the steering wheel.

Complementing these advances in technology is the advent of shared mobility platforms, leveraging digital tools to transform how we perceive ownership and accessibility. Shared mobility conjures images of ridesharing apps like Uber and Lyft, which ushered in an era where convenience and spontaneity reign. By efficiently utilizing existing vehicles, these platforms aim to alleviate congestion and offer mobility solutions that echo the public transit equity discussed earlier, albeit with the flexibility of personal transport.

Car-sharing and bike-sharing also belong in this ecosystem, introducing models where accessibility outweighs ownership. In bustling metropolises, they present sustainable options finely tuned to urban demands, with systems such as London's Santander Cycles and Car2Go offering scalable solutions amidst real estate constraints and environmental concerns. With mobility-as-a-service (MaaS) gaining momentum, cities are encouraged to integrate these platforms into larger transport networks, redefining how urban landscapes are navigated.

Lest we forget, the threads of emerging change extend beyond the terrestrial.   Skyward ventures envision air taxis and urban drones hovering above traffic entanglements, reshaping mobility with vertical dimensions. Fleeting notions ten years ago now edge towards practicality, with companies trialing prototypes in controlled environments.   While commonplace jetpacks might still dwell in the domain of dreams, innovations like electric vertical takeoff and landing (eVTOL) vehicles motivate us to look up, envisioning a cityscape buoyed by multiple layers of transit.

As fascinating as these technological visions might be, they spotlight a more significant narrative: the rethinking of mobility's fundamental fabric. Technological advances present tantalizing possibilities, but the alignment of policy, public acceptance, and equitable access will ultimately weave them into effective solutions. The annals of emerging mobility technology remind us that these innovations must harmonize with the public interest, ensuring that the crescendo of change results not just in progress, but prosperity for all.

Reflecting on the constellation of modern mobility— electric, autonomous, shared, and beyond—illuminates not just a path forward, but a constellation of potential. To harness this potential, urban stakeholders must consider the cultural shifts necessary to embrace these technologies and leverage them to uplift existing societal frameworks. For the tapestry of emerging technology is a tapestry of humanity—one that, if deftly crafted, promises to carry us towards a sustainable future that pulses with optimism.

Ultimately, the winds of change are invigorating our urban sails, challenging us to steer towards an unknown but promising horizon, where the landscape of mobility is rich with innovation, defined by inclusivity, and basks in sustainability. In this world, the journey is a harmonious play where technology and humanity unite, dancing in rhythm with the cities we call home.

4.5 Designing Walkable and Bike-Friendly Cities

Imagine stepping out into a city where the rhythm of footsteps and the harmonious whir of bicycles compose the soundtrack of urban life. Where streets echo not with honking horns, but with conversations and the rustle of leaves stirred by cyclists breezing past. This vision is not a utopian fantasy but rather a growing aspiration among urban planners and city dwellers alike—to craft environments that prioritize walking and cycling as principal modes of transport.

The seeds of walkable cities were sewn long ago in the narrow, winding streets of ancient towns, where walking was not merely an option but a necessity. Fast forward to the modern metropolis, and we encounter sprawling cities—notoriously car-centric—that often treat pedestrians and cyclists as afterthoughts. Yet, as realization dawns regarding sustainability and livability, cities are returning to their roots, discovering the profound benefits of designing for human rather than vehicular scales.

The foundational strategy for enhancing walkability is, quite literally, setting the stage: designing streets and public spaces that invite pedestrians with wide sidewalks, benches, and ample greenery. Copenhagen,

75

for instance, widely regarded as the gold standard, replaced its car-dominated streets with expansive pedestrian networks in the 1960s. The transformation has yielded vibrant urban corridors where pedestrians reign supreme, their presence fostered by pedestrian-only zones and interconnected plazas.

Parallel to pedestrian-friendly planning is the emergence of bike-friendly infrastructure, which recognizes that a bicycle is more than a mere two-wheeled contraption—it's a means of personal empowerment and environmental stewardship. The Netherlands has spearheaded this movement with a comprehensive network of dedicated bicycle lanes, prioritizing cyclists' safety by delineating their space with physical barriers and protected inter-sections. Resultantly, cycling in Dutch cities has tran-scended leisure, asserting itself as an integral fabric in the daily commuter tapestry.

Translating these successes to other cities entails a blend of infrastructure investment, policy incentives, and cultural shifts. At the heart of this trifecta is a planning ethos known colloquially as the "15-Minute City" concept, which aims to ensure that residents' essential needs—work, school, parks, and shops—are reachable within a quarter-hour walk or bike ride. This philosophical pivot nudges urban design towards holistic accessibility, encouraging the development of mixed-use neighborhoods where convenience and sustainability intersect.

Beyond the clay and mortar of city building lies a critical element: fostering a cycling and walking culture. This aspect encompasses efforts to recalibrate public perception, embracing walking and cycling not only as methods of transport but as lifestyle choices. Campaigns in cities like Minneapolis have embraced such narratives, normalizing cycling through public art, bike festivals, and community-led workshops, transforming perception from utility to identity.

Technology deftly underpins this cultural evolution, from app-based navigation systems identifying the safest routes for pedestrians and cyclists to bike-sharing platforms availing bicycles at the tap of a smartphone. By advancing connectivity, these tools significantly enhance urban dwellers' confidence to transition away from car dependency, with cities like Barcelona leveraging data-driven solutions to reduce cycling stress and streamline travel choices.

However, intrepid city designers must also grapple with the practical challenges of retrofitting existing urban infrastructures to accommodate these transformative ideas. Resistance invariably surfaces, often spearheaded by habitual drivers concerned about loss of lanes or parking. Here, change-makers borrow lessons from cities such as Bogotá, where temporary weekend road closures for "Ciclovía" provoke dialogues and enjoyment, demonstrating the benefits of change in a non-committal fashion.

Walkability and bikeability also yield lucrative benefits that stretch beyond transport. Real estate values can soar in areas where bicycles and pedestrian access are prioritized over cars, while local businesses witness increased foot traffic contributing directly to economic vibrancy. Cities, therefore, hold the potential to craft a symbiotic relationship where infrastructure investment fuels economic growth, thereby attracting further investment.

The resistors, of course, will point to justifiable challenges—weather constraints, crime, and varying terrain. Solutions to these are routed in innovative design: shade-resting areas combat summer heat, well-lit paths improve nighttime safety, and urban greenways weave through challenging landscapes, lovingly transforming obstacles into opportunities.

Cities of the future will likely grapple with a synthesis of virtual and physical spaces where technology shapes both pedestrian preferences and global connectivity. Yet, amid digital advances, the foundational need for tactile experiences—where one encounters the city directly, at human speed—remains unequivocal.

In this grand choreography of urban planning and policy innovation, designing walkable and bike-friendly cities presents an opportunity to pioneer a civilization more connected, serene, and sustainable. It invites us to imagine streets as places that people inhabit, enjoy, and traverse freely—unchaining society from the shackles of congestion while engendering vibrant, inclusive communities.

Thus, sculpting cities for walkers and pedal-pushers is more than an aesthetic undertaking—it is a transformative commitment to rewriting the narrative of urban life.

Chapter 5

Energy and Resource Efficiency

This chapter explores strategies for optimizing energy and re-source use in urban areas to promote sustainability. It covers the shift to renewable energy sources, energy-efficient building designs, and the role of smart grids in improving resource management. Emphasizing recycling and resource conservation, it highlights practices that reduce waste and environmental impact, contributing to sustainable urban living while addressing the demands of growing urban populations.

5.1 Understanding Energy Consumption in Cities

Urban areas are vibrant hubs of human activity and innovation, drawing people and resources from all corners of the globe. Yet, beneath this dynamism lies a complex web of energy consumption patterns that substantially impact our environment and society. As cities grow, understanding these patterns becomes not just beneficial, but essential, particularly in fostering sustainable urban development.

First, we delve into the nature of energy consumption in cities. Urban environments are characterized by their diverse and dense assembly of buildings, transportation networks, industries, and public spaces—all of which are voracious consumers of energy.   Historically, as cities expanded during the Industrial Revolution, they became epicenters of energy demand, initially fueled by coal and later by oil and natural gas. Today, cities account for over two-thirds of the world's energy use and more than 70% of global CO_2 emissions, making them crucial battlegrounds in the fight against climate change.

Energy use in cities is often categorized into four primary sectors: residential, commercial, industrial, and transportation. Each of these sectors contributes uniquely to the overall energy footprint of an urban area.   Residential and commercial buildings, for instance, consume energy for heating, cooling, and lighting. The advent of modern conveniences such as air conditioning and electric lighting in the 20th century increased residential electricity usage significantly. In contrast, the commercial sector tends to consume energy consistently across the day and night, driven by the needs of office buildings, retail outlets, and other business operations that thrive in urban settings.

The industrial sector is another major energy consumer, although its footprint varies depending on the city's economic profile. Cities with strong industrial bases tend to have higher energy demands owing to manufacturing processes, which can be energy-intensive. However, as cities evolve towards service-oriented economies, mechanized industry is often replaced by sectors like information technology, which, while still demanding, may reduce reliance on traditional energy sources.

Transportation is perhaps the most visibly impactful sector regarding urban energy consumption, intertwining with the city's spatial planning and infrastructure. The dependence on gasoline-powered vehicles has historically driven cities to expand with sprawling suburbs, creating an increased demand for energy as commuters travel into central urban areas. Public transit systems, while more energy-efficient, sometimes struggle to keep pace with population growth or infrastructural decay, compounding urban transportation challenges.

Efficiency across these sectors is critical. Unlike traditional, less efficient energy models, modern cities are increasingly looking towards more sustainable approaches. The motives here are both economic and environmental. From a financial perspective, energy-efficient practices lead to cost savings at various levels, from household energy bills to municipal budget allocations. Environmentally, enhancing efficiency reduces the carbon footprint and mitigates the urban heat island effect, a phenomenon where city centers become significantly warmer than their rural surroundings due to concentrated human activities and energy consumption.

An example of the critical role efficiency plays can be seen in energy auditing initiatives employed by numerous cities around the world. Take, for instance, New York City's "Greener, Greater Buildings Plan," which mandates that large buildings publicly report their energy use. Such transparency not only highlights inefficiencies but also encourages investment in energy conservation technologies.

Beyond individual interventions, urban planners must consider a holistic approach to energy use. Smart city technologies and the proliferation of the Internet of Things (IoT) provide pathways to managing urban energy consumption more intelligently. By integrating data from various sectors—like monitoring traffic flows, tracking electricity use in real time, or optimizing public transport routes—cities can better align their energy supply with peak demand periods, reducing waste and cost.

Another promising development is the increased incorporation of mixed-use zoning in urban planning, which aims to reduce transportation energy by situating residential areas closer to workplaces, thus cutting down commute times and energy use. The "15-minute city" concept embodies this trend, proposing urban areas where essential services can be reached within a short walk or bike ride.

Ultimately, cities represent both a challenge and opportunity in the pursuit of energy efficiency and sustainable development. They are microcosms of broader societal trends where population density, resource demands, and innovative solutions collide. Understanding energy use in these dynamic landscapes is crucial for developing strategies that not only accommodate urban growth but also safeguard our planet for future generations.

The sustainability of our urban future hinges on a nuanced understanding of energy consumption: a synthesis of historical evolution, current strategies, and future innovations. As cities continue to expand and transform, the opportunity for impactful change lies in our collective ability to harness energy efficiently and equitably.

5.2 Renewable Energy Sources

In the quest for sustainable urban living, renewable energy emerges as a beacon of hope—a transformative shift from traditional fossil fuels towards more sustainable and environmentally friendly alternatives. As our cities grow and the demand for energy intensifies, harnessing nature's power becomes both an economic and ecological imperative. This section delves into the transformative potential of renewable energy sources, such as solar, wind, and biomass, specifically within the urban context, providing a fresh perspective on how cities can sustain their growth without compromising the planet.

Solar energy, often hailed as the sun-drenched savior, provides an inexhaustible and clean energy source. Urban rooftops, displayed as blank canvases, hold vast potential for solar panels. These panels convert sunlight directly into electricity through photovoltaic (PV) cells. This not only reduces reliance on non-renewable energy but also empowers city dwellers to become proactive participants in their energy consumption. The installation of solar panels on city buildings—from residential homes to towering office blocks—has grown exponentially, driven by declining costs and increasing efficiency of solar technologies.

Beyond just the rooftops, innovative urban designs are increasingly incorporating solar technologies into building facades and even windows, providing both aesthetic and functional benefits. Imagine a skyscraper that doubles as a vertical solar farm—these are not just visions from a distant future but realities being constructed today. Cities like San Diego and Melbourne have led by example, boasting high rates of solar energy adoption, not only reducing energy costs but also creating resilience against the fluctuations of energy markets.

Complementing solar power, wind energy adds another layer to the urban renewable energy tapestry. While industrial-scale wind farms often find their home in rural areas, urban settings have begun to embrace smaller, building-integrated wind turbines. These turbines are designed to capture the high winds that play around skyscrapers and city structures. In doing so, they turn potential gusts into clean energy. High-rise buildings can be engineered to incorporate these turbines seamlessly into their designs, transforming architects' blueprints into practical solutions for energy independence.

Take the city of Rotterdam, for instance, where the "Windwheel" project conceptualizes a dual-functioning structure that serves both as a residential and commercial space while generating renewable energy through wind turbines integrated into its framework. Such innovative projects are peppering urban landscapes, redefining how cities perceive density and energy generation.

While wind and solar have received substantial attention, the urban potential of biomass should not be overlooked. Biomass refers to the organic materials, such as plant and animal waste, that can be used to produce energy. In cities, the steady stream of organic wastes—from dis-carded food and yard clippings to sewage—presents a golden opportunity to create energy through anaerobic digestion or fermentation processes. This not only pro-vides a renewable energy source but effectively reduces urban waste.

Developments in urban agriculture, such as vertical farms and community gardens, further bolster the potential for biomass energy. Cities like Stockholm have harnessed this potential through district heating networks powered partially by biomass energy, making strides in reusing what would otherwise be waste into a productive energy solution. This not only diversifies the cities' energy portfolios but also aligns with sustainable waste management practices.

Furthermore, policy and public initiatives play a pivotal

role in the adoption and integration of renewable energy in urban settings. Forward-thinking city planners and policymakers promote renewable energy through incentives, subsidies, and regulatory mandates. For instance, mandates for a certain percentage of energy to derive from renewable sources can propel cities towards cleaner futures. Publicly funded projects that install solar panels on public buildings or create energy-sharing programs in neighborhoods set powerful examples for citizens and catalyze community involvement.

However, transitioning to renewables in urban areas is not without its challenges. Spaces for large installations are limited, and navigating the urban governance structure can be complex. Yet, the integration of these energy sources offers not just a reduction in carbon emissions, but also a decentralization of energy production, making urban centers more robust against external shocks and blackouts.

Employment and economic opportunity also follow the trail blazed by these renewable energies. They generate green jobs in urban areas, from installation and maintenance of solar panels to engineering state-of-the-art wind and biomass systems. These sectors can invigorate urban economies, creating employment opportunities in traditionally sidelined communities.

In essence, the potential of renewable energy in urban environments is vast. Embracing these clean energy sources harmonizes with cities' goals of becoming more sustainable, resilient, and independent. The sun, the wind, and even urban waste hold the keys to powering our urban future. By integrating renewables, cities can thrive, not just today, but for generations to come, crafting environments that work with nature rather than against it. Here lies the embodiment of sustainability—an enduring promise of power drawn directly from the world around us, ever ready and endlessly renewable.

5.3   Energy-Efficient Building Designs

As cities continue to burgeon, consuming an ever-growing slice of the global energy pie, the buildings we construct and inhabit stand at the forefront of innovation in energy efficiency.   Crafting spaces that consume less energy fulfills twin goals: reducing environmental impact and cutting costs.   In this section, we explore how the principles of designing and retrofitting buildings for energy efficiency not only serve the planet but also enhance our urban experience.

Historically, the art of building has always adapted to its social and environmental milieu.   Ancient Roman structures cleverly utilized passive solar heating by orienting bathhouses to capture the sun's warmth, while traditional Middle Eastern homes incorporated wind towers and thick walls to remain cool in the searing heat.   Fast forward to the present, and the essence of these time-honored practices persists, albeit enhanced by contemporary technology and materials.

The   groundwork   for   energy-efficient   buildings rests on two key pillars: reducing energy demand through design and maximizing the efficiency of energy use through technology.   Let's first tackle the former.   Imagine architecture as a language; here, it speaks volumes through design decisions that diminish the need for artificial heating, cooling, and lighting. Orientation, for instance, is a primary design consideration. Buildings that skillfully harness sunlight during winter and shade during summer are invaluable in moderating internal temperatures.

Further, the building envelope, consisting of the roof,

walls, windows, and floors, plays a pivotal role in energy conservation. High-quality insulation, energy-efficient windows, and sealing air leaks help maintain desired indoor conditions, preventing unwanted heat transfer. Double-glazing and smart glass technology, for instance, have transformed windows from thermal weak points into strongholds of climate control. Meanwhile, roofing innovations like green roofs and cool roofs mitigate the urban heat island effect, reduce runoff, and provide natural insulation.

Moreover, architects and engineers have embraced renewable building materials that not only support energy savings but also emphasize sustainability. Materials like bamboo or reclaimed wood lighten the environmental burden of construction, while lightweight concrete mixed with insulating materials boosts the building's thermal mass and efficiency.

Technology further amplifies these gains in energy efficiency. Standing at the intersection of tradition and innovation is smart building management. Smart systems collect and analyze data to optimize heating, ventilation, and air conditioning (HVAC) use, adjusting to occupancy patterns and peak hours of energy use. Smart thermostats, such as the widely popular Nest system, learn user behavior to fine-tune energy use, providing comfort without waste.

Building automation systems (BAS) harness sensors and controls to coordinate lighting, indoor air quality, and temperature. Advanced BAS can reduce energy consumption by 10 to 25% while maintaining comfort and productivity for occupants. Meanwhile, LED lighting has reinvented illumination, offering significant savings over incandescent or fluorescent bulbs alongside longer life spans.

Beyond new constructions, the spectrum of retrofitting existing structures to be energy-efficient is as crucial as groundbreaking designs. Retrofitting often involves updating older buildings with more efficient HVAC systems, upgrading lighting, adding insulation, and possibly solar panels or other renewable energy solutions. From individual homes to iconic skyscrapers, successful retrofits breathe new life into aging infrastructures.

Consider the case of the Empire State Building, a legendary skyscraper in New York City. Its recent retrofit included replacing all 6,514 windows, upgrading the chiller plant controls, and installing reflective insulation. These measures have cut energy use by approximately 40%, setting a standard for similar landmarks worldwide.

While the technical aspects of these designs are compelling, they also weave into the human narrative. Creating energy-efficient spaces nurtures health and well-being by ensuring good air quality, abundant natural light, and comfortable climates. Biophilic design, which introduces natural elements into built environments, serves not only to save energy but also to enrich our psychological connection to nature, leading to happier and more productive occupants.

However, challenges remain. Regulatory frameworks, upfront costs, and the need for skilled professionals are hurdles that require navigation. Public policy is instrumental in overcoming these barriers. Incentives for energy-efficient retrofits, subsidies for renewable energy installations, and building codes mandating efficiency can accelerate adoption across the urban landscape.

Energy-efficient building design presents an exhilarating

blend of art, science, and sustainability. It invites us to reimagine urban spaces as living, breathing entities that coalesce both aesthetic beauty and functional brilliance. By shaping our structures with an eye towards energy conservation, we not only inhabit our cities but harmonize with them, laying the foundation for a resilient and sustainable future. Embarking on this journey, we honor a legacy of wisdom while embracing the promise of innovation—a testament to the profound impact of thoughtful design.

5.4 Smart Grids and Energy Management

The relentless hum of city life requires a vast and often invisible web of energy infrastructure, relentlessly working to keep the lights on, the trains running, and the myriad devices of our digital lives charged. Yet, this traditional power grid—an emblem of modernity—faces unprecedented challenges. As urban centers densify and expand, the quest for sustainable energy management rises to critical importance. Enter the smart grid: an innovative evolution of our energy systems designed to meet the demands of the 21st century with intelligence and flexibility.

A smart grid differs from its predecessor by embedding information technology into the energy system, threading a digital vein through the traditional wires and transformers. This digital transformation enables two-way communication between utilities and consumers, allowing for a more dynamic response to the ebbs and flows of energy demand.

To appreciate the revolutionary potential of smart grids, we must first consider the limitations of our legacy systems. Conventional energy grids are built upon outdated "predict-and-supply" models, where power generation is fixed and inflexible. This often leads to inefficiencies with surplus energy produced during low-demand periods and potential shortfalls during peak times. Moreover, these grids provide limited visibility into real-time usage and are vulnerable to disruptions ranging from natural disasters to cyber-attacks.

Smart grids, however, revolutionize this landscape with their capability for real-time monitoring and adaptive management of energy distribution. A smart grid can integrate diverse and distributed energy sources, deftly balancing the load through sophisticated algorithms. This juggling act allows for the seamless incorporation of renewable energy sources—like solar and wind—described earlier in this chapter. It is the intelligent architecture of smart grids that allows renewables to fulfill their promise, smoothing out the variability inherent in nature-driven power.

In the intricate dance of energy management, demand response is a key partner. Through a smart grid, utilities can incentivize customers to alter their power use patterns. For instance, consumers might reduce usage during high-demand periods in exchange for a discount, akin to receiving a golden ticket for a midnight snack from the energy factory. This dance optimizes existing resources and defers the need for expensive infrastructure investments.

Cities at the forefront of smart grid technology, such as Amsterdam and San Diego, showcase the benefits in action. In these locales, urban planners leverage smart grids to empower neighborhoods with microgrids—small-scale versions of the grid that operate independently or in conjunction with the main grid. These microgrids foster energy resilience and sustainability by incorporating local renewable energy sources and storage systems.

To dive deeper, consider a practical illustration of smart grids and energy management: the Brooklyn Microgrid project in New York. This community-based initiative enables peer-to-peer energy trading among neighbors using blockchain technology. Residents produce solar energy and sell excess power to their peers, forming a stable and locally-driven energy market. Such projects not only enhance energy security but also democratize energy ownership and inspire community engagement.

Furthermore, smart meters, the unsung heroes of smart grids, vastly improve energy management by monitoring energy consumption in real time. Armed with this detailed consumption data, both consumers and utilities can make more informed decisions. Households gain the power to identify energy-hogging appliances, adjust behaviors, and ultimately reduce their carbon footprints. Meanwhile, utilities gain insights to finely tune the supply-side.

The potential of smart grid technology extends its reach down to the level of smart appliances. Connecting washing machines, refrigerators, and thermostats to the grid network allows these devices to "talk" to the grid. Imagine receiving a text from your water heater, pleading to skoosh the heat up or down based on energy prices or available renewable energy—it's not the future but the now.

Yet, as illuminating as this technology may be, challenges remain. Implementing smart grids requires significant investment in infrastructure, cybersecurity enhancements, and a cooperative regulatory environment. Moreover, concerns about privacy and data security must be addressed to gain public trust and acceptance.

Conversely, the benefits of smart grids are vast, touching every corner of urban life. They pave the way for cleaner energy consumption by reducing reliance on fossil fuels. They enhance grid reliability, reducing outages and ensuring smoother recovery after disturbances. They cut peak energy loads and promote more efficient energy use, leading to economic savings for both cities and consumers.

Smart grids and modern energy management systems signify more than technological advancement—they represent a paradigm shift towards how we conceive and consume energy. By embracing innovation that interlaces technology with energy, we forge a path to urban sustainability that can serve our growing cities for decades ahead. Ultimately, the power lies in energy grids becoming not just providers of electricity, but intelligent allies in a collective quest for resilience and efficiency, nurturing our urban environments towards a balanced and sustainable future.

5.5   Efficient Resource Use and Recycling

The urban landscape, while stunningly efficient at fostering human activity, often mirrors the voracious appetite of an ever-hungry giant. With cities accounting for about 75% of natural resource consumption and waste production, their survival hinges on mastering the delicate dance of resource efficiency and recycling. Efficient resource use and recycling are twin virtues, not only reducing the environmental footprint but also revitalizing urban systems with their alchemy—of waste into worth, and scarcity into sufficiency.

As cities continue to grow, so does their demand for resources, from the concrete that lays their foundations to the water that sustains their populations. This brings us to a pivotal question: How can cities maximize the efficient use of resources whilst curtailing waste? One compelling approach lies in the circular economy—a model that fundamentally rethinks economic activities, converting the linear 'take-make-dispose' paradigm into a restorative cycle.

Circular economies emphasize designing out waste and pollution, keeping products and materials in use, and regenerating natural systems. In urban contexts, this involves creating loops in which the output of one process becomes the input for another, effectively transforming cities into self-sustaining entities. Imagine if buildings were designed with materials that, at the end of their life, could be disassembled and reused in new constructions. Such cradle-to-cradle thinking prolongs the life cycle of resources, reducing the need to extract new materials from the planet.

Recycling plays a cornerstone role in realizing this vision. It not only mitigates the need for virgin resources but also lowers energy consumption—recycling aluminum, for instance, saves up to 95% of the energy required to produce new aluminum from bauxite ore. Such practices are vital in city strategies to manage waste sustainably. Yet, urban recycling programs must evolve beyond the mundane to achieve meaningful impact.

A shining beacon on this path is San Francisco's Zero Waste program, aiming to divert all waste from landfills by 2025 through comprehensive recycling and composting initiatives. This includes robust educational campaigns, effective sorting infrastructure, and forward-thinking policies. Such cities illustrate that with concerted effort, vibrant urban landscapes can coexist with exhaustive waste management practices.

However, resource efficiency is not solely about recycling old materials; it also involves rethinking how we design and consume products in the first place. Eco-design, or designing with environmental considerations in mind, pushes for creating products that are durable, repairable, and upgradable. This slower rhythm of consumption emphasizes quality and longevity over disposable convenience.

Besides design, innovative technologies are revolutionizing how resources are used in cities. Consider smart water systems that detect leaks in real time, akin to a digital network of eyes and ears that reduce water waste. Furthermore, symbiotic industrial practices, where waste heat from one plant powers another, redefine efficiency by finding value in what once was disregarded.

Digital technologies also drive resource efficiency through sharing economies, which reduce the burden of ownership. Urbanites increasingly embrace platforms that provide as-needed access to cars, tools, and even living spaces, reducing resource intensity across the board. Peer-to-peer sharing systems, empowered by apps, allow residents to seamlessly access resources, minimizing the demand for new products.

While technology serves as a powerful ally, community engagement remains integral to changing consumption patterns. Urban planners and policymakers can foster environments where citizens partake in resource efficiency as stakeholders, not just bystanders. When individuals buy into community-based recycling programs or participate in local markets for exchanging goods, the ripple effect empowers sustainable urban resource cycles.

Education further fortifies this transformation. It imbues citizens with a sense of ownership and responsibility, fostering a culture of conservation. Teaching young minds about resource efficiency and recycling integrates these values as second nature. Imagine educational curriculums that challenge students to design projects centered around sustainability, inspiring real-world applications of theoretical concepts.

That being said, challenges abound. Efficient resource use and recycling in cities necessitate overcoming infrastructural, behavioral, and policy-based barriers. Ineffective sorting systems or insufficient recycling facilities can stymie progress. Policies that incentivize linear consumption must be unraveled and replaced with frameworks that reward sustainability.

Nevertheless, cities around the world are stepping up to overcome these hurdles. In Japan, the "mottainai" ethos—which translates to a sense of regret over waste— is deeply ingrained, influencing policy and personal behaviors alike. Japanese cities efficiently transform organic waste into biogas, cleverly closing loops within the urban ecosystem.

By embracing a holistic approach to resource efficiency and recycling, cities embark on a journey towards resilience and sustainability. This transformation involves more than merely adding another bin to the garbage collection—it requires reimagining lifestyles, systems, and economies. Cities, as epicenters of innovation and cultural shifts, wield the power to craft an urban future where efficient resource use and recycling are not only norms but celebrated virtues. As we re-chart this course, every redesigned product, recycled material, and conserved resource lights a path to transformations—ensuring urban prosperity and ecological balance for generations to come.

Chapter 6

Sustainable Water and Waste Management

This chapter addresses urban challenges in water conservation and waste management by outlining innovative techniques like rainwater harvesting, greywater recycling, and modern waste management practices. It discusses waste-to-energy technologies and the critical role of community participation in reducing waste. By adopting sustainable practices, cities can manage resources more effectively, minimize environmental impact, and enhance the quality of urban life.

6.1 Urban Water Challenges

Urban areas worldwide are no strangers to water-related challenges, which manifest in various forms such as scarcity and pollution. These issues are not mere hiccups in municipal planning; they are deep-rooted challenges that threaten the very sustainability of cities. Understanding the intricacies of these challenges requires not just a glance at modern and historical contexts but also an exploration of their implications on urban life.

The problem of water scarcity is perhaps one of the most pressing issues. Picturing a bustling metropolis, one often envisions towers of glass and steel, perhaps

accompanied by the comforting sound of water flowing
in fountains or canals. Yet, beneath this veneer, many
cities teeter on the edge of a different reality—one
where water scarcity threatens their growth and
survival. Water scarcity itself arises not just from the
physical absence of water but also due to economic
and infrastructural hurdles that limit access to available
resources.

Arid regions naturally face more pressing scarcity
issues, such as parts of the Middle East and North
Africa where rainfall is minimal. However, sprawling
urban centers in more temperate climates can also face
issues due to overpopulation, inadequate infrastructure,
and unsustainable consumption patterns. For instance,
Los Angeles, despite its proximity to the ocean, wrestles
with acute water scarcity due to its semi-arid climate,
large population, and the environmental stressors
induced by climate change.

Scarcity is further compounded by pollution, which diminishes the quantity of water available for consumption. Polluted waterways can be attributed to industrial
effluents, agricultural runoff, and inefficient waste disposal practices, often poisoning the well, quite literally,
for cities. One illustrative account is the Ganges River
in India, a source of sustenance for millions, yet heavily
polluted with industrial waste, sewage, and religious of-
ferings. The indelible impact of such contamination extends beyond environmental degradation, affecting human health, aquatic life, and the broader ecosystem.

In navigating these challenges, cities must confront the
historical legacies that have shaped their water policies
and infrastructures. Historically, urban water management has revolved around engineering feats—consider
Roman aqueducts or the intricate canal systems in pre-
modern China. These systems sought to control water

and deliver it efficiently, yet often at immense environmental costs, disrupting natural water flows and altering
landscapes.

Modern urban challenges demand a paradigm shift
from control and exploitation to sustainability and
resilience. Technology and science offer a glimpse
into the future with innovations such as smart water
systems capable of detecting leaks and automating
water distribution to minimize wastage. Moreover,
advances in water purification technology promise to
reclaim usable water even from highly contaminated
sources. These tools are essential in cities like Cape
Town, which grapple with 'Day Zero' scenarios when
city reservoirs run dry.

Yet, technology alone is not a panacea. Resolving
urban water challenges requires a holistic approach
that includes robust policy frameworks, infrastructural
investment, and community engagement. Governance
plays a critical role here; policies that prioritize
sustainable water usage and ensure equitable
distribution are paramount. Public awareness
campaigns can empower communities to adopt water-
saving habits, a grassroots effort that can significantly
reduce the demand burden. Singapore serves as a
paragon by employing a 'four national tap' strategy
consisting of imported water, local catchments, recycled
NEWater, and desalinated water, showcasing an
integrated approach towards water security.

As we parse through the layers of urban water
challenges, it becomes evident that addressing them is
not an isolated task but a collective endeavor embracing
innovation, stringent policy-making, and active citizen
participation. Moving forward into a more sustainable
urban era necessitates bending the arc of history towards
smart and inclusive water management solutions.

6.2   Water Conservation Techniques

As urban centers burgeon and water resources grow
scarcer, innovative conservation techniques become
not merely advantageous but essential. Cities, often
finding themselves caught in a hydraulic vice grip,
must adopt strategies that mitigate wastage and bolster
reserves. This section delves into the creative arsenal at
the disposal of urban planners and citizens alike, with
an emphasis on two powerhouse techniques: rainwater
harvesting and greywater recycling.

Starting with rainwater harvesting, this approach taps
into the natural rhythm of precipitation. By collecting
and storing rainwater, cities transform a simple, often
discarded resource into a vital component of their water supply. Historically, civilizations have appreciated
the value of rainwater. The ancient Romans, clever architects and planners, utilized extensive systems of cis-
terns to capture rainfall, ensuring that every drop was
used during dry spells. Similarly, cultures in India have
long practiced rainwater harvesting through stepwells
and baolis, showcasing an implicit understanding of the
seasonal dance of water.

Modern adaptations of rainwater harvesting techniques
are both technologically advanced and widely accessible,
allowing even individual households to partake. On the
simplest level, homeowners can place barrels beneath
downspouts, collecting runoff for non-potable uses like
gardening or flushing toilets. At a more sophisticated
scale, urban designs incorporate larger catchment systems, linking them with infrastructure to feed rainwater
directly into municipal supplies. This not only provides
alternative sources but also reduces strain on stormwater systems, curbing urban flood risks. Cities like Melbourne and Berlin have championed such practices, inte-

grating rooftop gardens and permeable pavements that funnel water to underground repositories.

Pivoting towards greywater recycling, this practice capitalizes on another undervalued resource. Greywater—wastewater from sinks, baths, and washing machines—can, when appropriately processed, be repurposed for uses such as irrigation or toiletry flushes. Unlike its dirtier counterpart, blackwater, which requires more intensive treatment, greywater can be reclaimed with relatively simple filtration systems. Israel, a leading advocate in water conservation, employs this technique extensively, treating greywater for agricultural irrigation, contributing significantly to the nation's heavy emphasis on water reuse.

In practical terms, greywater systems can range from domestic installations, where simple filters are connected to household water systems, to industrial-scale operations integrated with city-wide sewage networks. An exemplary case is California, where prolonged droughts have necessitated rigorous water-saving measures. Here, greywater systems are increasingly common in new building developments; state codes even encourage their implementation by providing guidelines and incentives.

The truth behind the potency of these techniques lies not just in technological promise but in their societal integration. Water conservation efforts require broad-based awareness and engagement from urban dwellers. Education plays a pivotal role in this integration, fostering a culture where the conservation of water becomes second nature. Interestingly, the global shift toward smart cities has helped propel these practices into the limelight. The marriage of technology and sustainability allows for the real-time monitoring of water usage, encouraging homeowners and businesses to adopt conservation measures and track their effectiveness. For instance, Singapore's national campaign includes smart meters that provide instantaneous feedback on water consumption, empowering users to make more informed choices.

Nevertheless, like any endeavour, challenges persist. Initial setup costs for rainwater harvesting systems or greywater networks can deter uptake, especially in regions where immediate incentives are unclear. Moreover, misinformation regarding the safety and effectiveness of these methods can fuel resistance. This is where leadership shines, showcasing transitions from concept to norm, much like Australia's shift post-millennium drought to incorporate rainwater tanks in residential building codes, or Tokyo's unyielding pursuit of rainwater utilization projects.

Water conservation is a collective and ongoing effort, reliant on the seamless interplay of innovation, policy, and public participation. By embracing techniques like rainwater harvesting and greywater recycling, cities position themselves not only to confront but to conquer the challenges posed by dwindling water supplies. Therein lies the true efficacy of these practices—not merely in water saved but in the legitimate proof that urban resilience, once a lofty ideal, is firmly within reach.

6.3 Modern Waste Management Practices

In the vibrant tapestry of urban life, waste is an inevitable thread. The modern cityscape pulsates with the constant hum of consumption and, consequently, the inevitable byproduct: waste. From heaps of trash to emissions and electronic refuse, cities face a persistent challenge in managing what they discard. But what if waste were not the bane of modern existence but rather a hidden resource waiting to be tapped?

Such is the allure of modern waste management practices, wherein sophisticated systems and enlightened strategies aim to transmute urban refuse into opportunities for resource recovery and environmental stewardship. This section explores these transformative approaches, paving the way for cleaner, greener urban environments.

To unravel the complexities of contemporary waste management, it's instructive to first glance backwards. Throughout history, waste disposal was often an afterthought—pits, rivers, or the distant outskirts of settlements traditionally bore the brunt of humanity's discarded materials. This haphazard approach, however, led to myriad problems, from public health crises to the polluting of land and waterways. Cities like 19th-century London, for instance, were infamous for their sanitation woes, giving rise to miasmas and disease outbreaks, spurring the Victorian obsession with cleanliness.

Fast forward to today, where waste management has evolved into a sophisticated discipline, pivoting around the principles of reduce, reuse, and recycle. At its core, modern waste management stresses the importance of minimizing waste generation at the source. This proactive stance begins at the consumer level, encouraging designs that are eco-efficient, biodegradable, or recyclable.

Once waste is generated, contemporary systems emphasize recycling and composting to recover usable resources. This process requires the sorting of waste into distinct categories: organic, recyclable, and residual. San Francisco, for example, boasts an impressive waste diversion rate, thanks in part to regulations that mandate recycling and composting while prohibiting certain materials in landfills. Implementing citywide sorting systems can significantly reduce the volume directed toward landfills, thus mitigating the environmental footprint.

Innovations in waste processing further enhance these efforts. Technologies such as mechanical biological treatment (MBT) and anaerobic digestion (AD) convert organic waste into energy. MBT facilities sort and treat waste, often producing refuse-derived fuel (RDF) for energy generation or compost for soil enrichment. Anaerobic digestion, on the other hand, involves the breakdown of organic materials by microorganisms in the absence of oxygen. The result is biogas, a versatile energy source that can replace fossil fuels.

Let's not overlook the pivotal role of waste-to-energy (WtE) technologies, which elevate waste from nuisance to nourishment. WtE processes burn refuse to generate heat, which is then used to produce electricity. Countries like Sweden exemplify this transition, importing others' waste to fuel their national energy grid, testament to the efficiency of their systems and the diminishing stigma around waste treatment.

Yet, as promising as these technologies are, modern waste management systems confront an array of challenges. Navigating the complexities of waste requires not just cutting-edge technologies but also a symbiotic relationship between individuals, businesses, and governance. Public education initiatives must underscore the collective benefit derived from conscientious waste disposal and recycling habits. Moreover, the integration of policy frameworks that incentivize sustainable practices and penalize infractions is crucial for maintaining momentum. The

European Union's Circular Economy Action Plan, which outlines initiatives to reduce waste while stimulating sustainable growth, serves as an archetype of robust governance.

Compounding these efforts, logistic advancements in smart waste management offer a glimpse into the future. Smart waste bins equipped with sensors and Internet of Things (IoT) technology optimize collection routes, reducing emissions and operational costs. Cities like Amsterdam have adopted these innovations, demonstrating that coupling technology with urban planning can markedly enhance efficiency.

Ultimately, modern waste management is not merely about discarding less; it is about envisioning waste as a multidimensional opportunity. The shift from linear to circular economies signals a promising trajectory, where materials are perpetually cycled through the economy rather than meeting premature ends in landfills.

While the challenge of waste remains a fixture in urban life, contemporary strategies offer compelling solutions. The key lies in embracing an assortment of approaches, reinforcing policies with education and innovation, and transforming waste into an integral player in the fabric of urban sustainability. As cities continue to grow and evolve, so too must their waste management practices—casting waste not as the residue of progress, but as a springboard to a more sustainable future.

6.4 The Role of Waste-to-Energy Technologies

In the grand narrative of urbanization, waste has long been cast as a villain. Yet, in the age of technology and sustainability, we find ourselves rewriting the script.

Enter waste-to-energy (WtE) technologies, the unsung heroes poised to turn the tide, converting our refuse into a resourceful ally. This transformation not only helps manage waste but also contributes significantly to the energy mix, offering a compelling solution to urban sustainability challenges.

At its core, waste-to-energy technology encompasses a variety of processes to generate energy from waste. Historically, the concept is not entirely new—humans have utilized basic forms of burning waste for warmth and light for centuries. However, the refinement of these processes has propelled WtE technologies into a sophisticated realm of energy production today.

The environmental promise of WtE lies in its dual capacity to solve two pressing urban dilemmas: waste management and energy generation. By incinerating waste in a controlled environment, these plants produce heat, which is then converted into electricity. This not only reduces the volume of waste by up to 90%, significantly easing the burden on landfills, but also generates renewable energy, contributing to urban energy demands.

Consider Sweden, a pioneer in the WtE domain, which has seamlessly integrated this technology into its national energy strategy. With 34 waste-to-energy plants, Sweden has not only achieved a drastic reduction in landfill dependency but also imports waste from neighboring countries to fuel its plants. This practice is as much about energy production as it is about resourceful economic exchange. The Swedes have demonstrated an admirable knack for turning another nation's trash into their treasure, producing heat for hundreds of thousands of homes in the process.

The practical execution of WtE, however, is not without its challenges. Emissions, for instance, are a traditional concern associated with incineration. Modern WtE facilities must therefore adhere to stringent emission standards, employing sophisticated filtration systems and scrubbing technologies to curtail harmful outputs. When executed correctly, the emissions are often significantly lower than those from traditional fossil fuel-based power plants, aligning closely with urban sustainability goals.

In addition to incineration, WtE encompasses several mechanical and biological processes to recover energy from waste. Anaerobic digestion, for example, is a vital WtE process particularly adept at treating organic waste. By leveraging microbial processes in the absence of oxygen, anaerobic digestion not only diminishes organic output but produces biogas—a versatile energy source. Cities like Copenhagen have harnessed such methodologies, showcasing biogas as a clean alternative to power their public transport systems.

Gasification and pyrolysis are other promising WtE technologies, operating at higher temperatures to convert waste into syngas—a synthesis gas usable for generating electricity or as a building block for producing synthetic fuels. These methods hold particular promise due to their flexibility and potential for high efficiency in energy recovery.

Nevertheless, the expansion and scaling of WtE facilities require careful planning and robust policy support. Public perception challenges, often rooted in concerns over emissions and health risks, must be addressed through transparency and education. Moreover, economic considerations, such as the initial capital investment and operating costs, need evaluation against the backdrop of potential environmental and energy savings.

Governments have a crucial role in fostering WtE

adoption, not merely as providers of regulatory
oversight but as champions of sustainable innovation.
Incentives for incorporating green technologies, clear
emissions guidelines, and public-private partnerships
for plant operations can nurture the growth of this
sector. The European Union, for instance, stands
at the forefront of this movement, embedding WtE
within broader strategies like the circular economy
framework, which prioritizes resource efficiency and
waste minimization.

As urban landscapes continue to evolve, the strategic
implementation of WtE can serve multiple urban needs.
Not only does it represent a feasible path to managing
the ever-growing mountains of waste, but it also ably
supplements renewable energy portfolios, thereby
reducing reliance on fossil fuels. The energy derived
from waste contributes to energy security, aiding cities
in navigating the turbulence of global energy markets
and fluctuating resource availability.

Waste-to-energy technologies encapsulate a dynamic
intersection between waste management and energy
generation. By addressing the dual challenge of waste
disposal and renewable energy production, WtE has
cemented itself as a cornerstone of sustainable urban
development. The ingenuity of turning waste into watts
serves as more than just an environmental solution;
it is a testament to human resilience and innovation,
showcasing the steadfast pursuit of harmony between
progress and preservation. In this continually unfolding
narrative of urbanization, waste has found redemption,
writing itself anew as a beacon of possibility in paving
the path to sustainability.

6.5 Community Participation in Waste Reduction

In the multifaceted quest for sustainable cities, community participation in waste reduction emerges as a lively symphony, where each note—each citizen— plays a crucial part in harmonizing the urban landscape. Beyond the towers of technology and policy lies a more grassroots yet equally vital component: the power of people. Harnessing this power, communities worldwide are stepping up to steer urban areas toward a cleaner, more sustainable future. Understanding this dynamic requires appreciating the historical context of community engagement and recognizing the exciting contemporary movements reshaping waste reduction practices.

Historically, the idea of community-based waste reduction may conjure images of neighborhood clean-ups or local recycling drives. These community efforts are not new—in fact, they date back to post-industrial revolutions when urbanization brought about visible refuse on city streets, spurring communities into collective action. Residents took matters into their own hands, organizing waste removal or advocating for municipal services. Such initiatives laid the groundwork for modern community involvement in urban environmental stewardship.

Today, the call for community participation resonates louder than ever, but with sophisticated undertones. As cities grow and waste piles up, local action becomes indispensable. Consider Japan, where community involvement in waste sorting has become a cultural norm. Japan's meticulous waste segregation system owes its success to strict compliance by citizens, who meticulously sort waste into upwards of a dozen categories.   This process is ingrained from childhood, underscoring the idea that waste reduction starts at home.

The beauty of community participation lies in its accessibility and adaptability.   Anyone can take part, often starting with small lifestyle changes that collectively make a significant impact.   Think of the zero-waste movement, which has grown from a fringe idea to a mainstream lifestyle change, advocating for eliminating personal waste.   Communities worldwide have embraced concepts such as bulk buying, using reusable containers, and composting, reducing waste at the source and diminishing the demand on municipal systems.

Education and empowerment are pivotal to these efforts. Knowledge-sharing initiatives, such as workshops or informational campaigns, equip citizens with the know-how to reduce waste.   Portland, Oregon, offers an illuminating example with its Master Recycler program—a hands-on course teaching residents about waste reduction, recycling, and sustainable living practices. These graduates become community leaders, helping spread awareness and practical solutions throughout their neighborhoods, creating ripples of change.

Motivating community involvement requires more than just education; it requires a shared vision and tangible benefits.   Incentive-based programs serve as powerful catalysts in galvanizing local action.   Pay-as-you-throw (PAYT) schemes, implemented in cities like Seoul, charge households based on the amount of waste they discard, encouraging them to generate less.   The economic incentive aligns personal habits with broader ecological goals, reinforcing responsible waste practices.

Community gardens also highlight the intersection of sustainability and social benefit. By reclaiming vacant urban land, these gardens transform spaces into vibrant hubs for ecological education, local food production, and organic waste recycling. They serve as living classrooms where the principles of waste reduction come to life—literally and metaphorically. Residents learn to compost organic waste, feeding the cycle of growth while reducing what ends up in landfills.

In the digital age, technology extends the reach and impact of community efforts. Mobile apps and social media platforms facilitate information-sharing, coordination, and collective action. Initiatives like Litterati—a global app encouraging individuals to photograph and map litter—foster a sense of global community participation. The data collected validates the efforts and provides valuable insights for city planners and environmental organizations.

Of course, the journey is not without challenges. Barriers such as apathy, misinformation, and resource limitations can hinder progress. To overcome these, local governments play a crucial role in supporting community initiatives through clear policies, funding, and infrastructure. Public-private partnerships, as seen with Finland's Sitra Foundation, can provide essential support, helping bridge gaps and amplify community projects.

Despite these challenges, the potential for communities to lead the waste reduction charge remains vast. As people increasingly recognize their shared role in sustainability, they gain the tools to drive transformative change. Community engagement becomes the heartbeat of urban waste management, offering resilience and adaptability in the face of growing environmental challenges.

The fusion of community participation and waste reduction represents a paradigm shift—a realization that when citizens unite, they possess the power to redefine urban landscapes. By fostering local initiatives, cultivating eco-conscious mindsets, and creatively employing technology, we can rewrite the urban narrative, crafting cities that are not only sustainable but also richly interconnected ecosystems. The future of urban waste reduction rests not merely in grand strategies but in the hands of the communities, charting a collaborative course towards a cleaner, brighter tomorrow.

Chapter 7

Green Spaces and Urban Biodiversity

This chapter highlights the benefits of urban green spaces and biodiversity for enhancing quality of life and ecological balance. It covers strategies for designing parks and natural areas, promoting urban biodiversity, and supporting urban agriculture. Addressing challenges in maintaining greenery, it emphasizes the importance of integrating nature into cities to foster resilient ecosystems, improve air quality, and provide spaces for recreation and community building.

7.1 Benefits of Urban Green Spaces

Imagine strolling through a bustling city center, where towering skyscrapers cast shadows over the concrete jungle. Suddenly, you arrive at a vibrant park, an oasis of green amidst the gray. Birds chirp harmoniously, children giggle with glee, and people of all ages laugh, relax, and recharge. This captivating scene highlights the invaluable role of urban green spaces as beacons of social interaction, environmental health, and economic vitality.

In the modern urban landscape, green spaces have evolved from simple aesthetic embellishments to crucial components of infrastructure, significantly enriching

113

the quality of human life and ecological balance.

A Social Elixir

Green spaces provide a much-needed remedy for the rapid pace of urban life. Among their foremost social contributions, they serve as inclusive public arenas where diverse communities converge. Parks and gardens play host to a myriad of activities—be it family picnics, community events, or solitary reflections—thereby fostering a sense of community and belonging. In these shared spaces, interactions break down perceived barriers and build robust social networks. The therapeutic effect of nature also enhances mental well-being, offering urban-dwellers an escape to tranquility amidst urban chaos.

Moreover, green spaces offer platforms for physical activities, promoting healthier lifestyles. They invite urbanites to embrace active transportation options like walking and cycling, which can otherwise be challenging on city streets. By nurturing physically active communities, green spaces become integral to public health strategies, combating lifestyle-induced ailments like obesity and heart diseases.

Environmental Boons

While their social benefits are evident, urban green spaces also execute vital environmental functions. These patches of greenery transform cities into more sustainable habitats, acting as the earth's lungs—absorbing carbon dioxide and releasing oxygen. They naturally filter air pollutants, improving urban air quality and reducing respiratory illnesses. Additionally, urban vegetation mitigates the urban heat island effect, wherein cities become significantly warmer than their rural counterparts due to human activities and infrastructure. By providing shade and cooling, green

114

spaces help moderate local climates and alleviate the burden on energy systems.

Beneath the surface, green spaces enhance soil quality, promote water retention, and reduce the risk of flooding by facilitating natural drainage. This becomes increasingly critical as climate change brings about unpredictable weather patterns and intensified rainfall. Through these functions, green spaces contribute to the resilience of cities against environmental challenges, ensuring they remain habitable in a changing world.

Economic Enrichment

Apart from social and environmental dividends, green spaces yield substantial economic benefits. Property values in proximity to parks and verdant areas consistently outpace those further removed from such amenities. Beyond residential appeal, commercial spaces nearby also profit from increased foot traffic due to the attraction of a lush environment, boosting local economies.

In the long term, the economic implications extend to reduced healthcare costs. By facilitating active lifestyles and improving air quality, urban green spaces contribute to healthier populations, leading to less strain on medical services. Furthermore, they catalyze job creation, not only through their maintenance and development but also by fostering spaces where urban agriculture can thrive. Community gardens, for instance, offer local employment opportunities and promote food security with fresh, local produce.

Historical Context and Evolution

The acknowledgment of green spaces is not a new phenomenon. Historically, urban green areas have been part of city planning from as early as the Renaissance, emphasizing the harmonious integration of nature and architecture. Famous examples include New York's Central Park, designed in the mid-19th century, which transformed a swath of urban continent into a flourishing public park serving millions each year. These historical green spaces were set up as retreats for urban inhabitants, but their roles have since expanded, aligning with contemporary priorities of sustainability and livability.

The evolution of green spaces has also seen innovative approaches in urban planning, such as the green belt movements and the creation of linear parks along rivers or abandoned railway lines. These efforts demonstrate a shift towards multifunctional and accessible green infrastructure, accommodating evolving urban demands while respecting the diversity of natural ecosystems.

Towards a Greener Tomorrow

Despite evident merits, the integration of green spaces in urban planning can face challenges related to political will, funding, and available space. Addressing these requires visionary strategies and an appreciation for the value of green spaces as potent urban solutions rather than mere embellishments.

Communities and policymakers alike recognize the need to prioritize green spaces within the tapestry of urban living. They are the sinews that knit the urban fabric together, creating cities that not only endure environmental stressors but flourish under them. As we advance into the 21st century, the expansion and innovation of urban green spaces stand as a testament to human commitment to balance development with ecological stewardship.

The next time one finds themselves enjoying the serenity of a city park, it is worth pondering not only the joys these spaces bring but also the myriad benefits they bestow upon our societies, economies, and environments. Indeed, urban green spaces are the verdant veins that sustain the vibrant life of cities.

7.2 Designing Parks and Natural Areas in Cities

Creating a patch of nature in the heart of a bustling city might seem like a magical endeavor, but it is, in reality, a delicate dance involving both art and science. The design of urban parks and natural spaces is a thoughtful process that seeks to imbue concrete landscapes with vibrant life, creating sanctuaries that offer both beauty and utility.

Principles of Urban Green Design

The process of designing urban parks is underpinned by several key principles that ensure these spaces cater to the diverse needs of city residents and ecosystems alike. One core principle is accessibility; parks should be easily reachable for all city dwellers, regardless of age or ability. This means integrating green spaces into the urban grid in ways that connect them seamlessly with public transport and pedestrian pathways.

Another guiding principle is inclusivity. Urban parks must foster environments where people of all backgrounds can gather, enjoy, and participate in activities. This involves designing multifunctional spaces that cater to different recreational needs, from tranquil walking paths for reflection to vibrant play areas for children and sports facilities for enthusiasts.

Moreover, the principle of sustainability is paramount. Green spaces should not only serve current generations but also be enduring, requiring designs that thrive with minimal intervention while enhancing biodiversity, efficiently managing resources like water, and supporting native plant and animal species.

Strategies for Effective Design

To bring these principles to life, designers employ various strategies. One common approach is the use of biophilic design, which seeks to create a deep connection between humans and nature through architecture and landscape. This might involve using natural materials, fostering views of greenery, or creating gradients of vegetation that echo natural ecosystems.

To maximize space in dense urban environments, designers often opt for vertical gardens or green roofs, transforming walls and rooftops into thriving natural habitats. These innovations not only expand the available green space but also help insulate buildings, reducing energy costs and enhancing air quality.

A rapidly emerging strategy is the creation of green corridors—linear parks or trails that link disparate green pockets into an interconnected network. These corridors not only facilitate the movement of people and wildlife but also actively engage communities by providing continuous recreational routes for cycling or walking.

Historical Context: Parks as Democratic Spaces

Urban parks have historically been envisioned as democratic spaces—grounds where the social distinctions of city life dissolve. Originating in the 19th century, public parks like Central Park in New York were explicitly designed as egalitarian refuges from industrial excess. The legacy of this vision is seen today in the expectation that parks facilitate social cohesion and nurture urban communities.

Designers today draw on this rich history, but with modern enhancements. For example, public feedback during the design process has become an invaluable tool, ensuring that new parks meet the evolving needs of varied user groups. This not only democratizes the design but ensures parks remain relevant and beloved by their communities.

Applications and Examples

A stunning example of ingenious park design is the High Line in New York City. What was once an elevated railway has been transformed into a linear park, weaving through the cityscape and offering stunning views and diverse ecological exhibits. The linear design encourages exploration while serving as a thriving habitat for urban biodiversity.

London's Queen Elizabeth Olympic Park similarly illustrates the transformative power of thoughtful design. Initially created for the 2012 Olympic Games, the park has been developed into a dynamic public space that hosts international sporting events, festivals, and community gatherings, underpinned by landscapes that promote ecological diversity and sustainability.

Challenges and Opportunities

Despite the ambitious vision and innovation driving park design, challenges persist. Urban land is a precious commodity, and space allocated for parks often competes with other critical infrastructure needs. Funding can also be a significant hurdle, as maintenance and development costs necessitate creative financing solutions.

However, these challenges present potent opportunities. The integration of technology allows for smarter, more resilient designs. Sensors and data analytics can monitor soil moisture, detect pollution levels, and even track park usage patterns, enabling tailored maintenance and programming.

Furthermore, there is a growing recognition of the economic value parks bring, from boosting property values to attracting tourism and catalyzing local business growth. By framing parks as essential infrastructure capable of delivering economic returns, designers and planners can make compelling cases for increasing urban green space investments.

The Future of Urban Green Spaces

As cities aspire to become more resilient, sustainable, and inclusive, urban park design will undoubtedly play a crucial role. Design approaches must continue to evolve, integrating more community-led initiatives and scaling with urban expansion. These green gems in cityscapes promise not only to enrich urban lives but to embody a commitment to future-ready living environments.

Designing parks and natural areas in cities is much more than planting trees and laying pathways. It is about fostering spaces that echo the vibrancy, diversity, and dynamism of the urban tapestry itself. As stakeholders increasingly realize the profound impact these spaces have on human and environmental health, the momentum for expanding and innovating urban green spaces appears unstoppable—and wholly necessary for crafting cities that are as nurturing as they are enduring.

7.3 Enhancing Biodiversity in Urban Landscapes

Picture a day in the city where the melody of birdsong competes with the hum of traffic, bees dance across balconies, and butterflies alight on blooming rooftop gardens. This is not a scene from a utopian vision but an achievable reality through the enhancement of biodiversity in urban landscapes. Biodiversity, the kaleidoscope of life in all its forms, is crucial for resilient ecosystems, and nurturing it within cities is an intriguing challenge that combines innovation, ecology, and community spirit.

The Urban Jungle: A New Wildlife Haven

Understanding urban landscapes as potential wildlife havens requires a shift in perspective. Cities, often seen as biotic wastelands, can become thriving ecosystems if we consciously create and connect habitats. The mosaic of parks, gardens, green roofs, and urban farms, if designed thoughtfully, can offer ample opportunities for diverse species to thrive amid human habitation.

One technique for enhancing urban biodiversity involves developing multifunctional green spaces. These areas not only provide recreational and aesthetic benefits but also support various species. Incorporating native vegetation is particularly effective, as these plants have evolved to suit the local climate and soil conditions while offering food and habitat to native fauna. This strategy supports a self-sustaining environment where organisms interact naturally.

Strategic Habitat Creation

An innovative strategy is the creation of wildlife corridors—pathways that allow species to migrate safely through urban areas. These corridors can range

121

from tree-lined streets to purpose-built green bridges over busy roads. By connecting fragmented habitats, they ensure genetic diversity and viable populations of urban wildlife.

The restoration of waterways and the creation of green buffers along riverbanks is another critical step. These riparian zones are rich in biodiversity, providing habitats for species that otherwise struggle amidst urban sprawl. In cities with water bodies, simple measures such as reducing concrete embankments can transform sterile urban waterways into vibrant ecological corridors.

For practical application, one can look to Singapore's transformation initiatives, which aim to reconcile urban development with ecological preservation. With projects like the Bishan-Ang Mo Kio Park, the city exemplifies how softened urban streams and lush plantings can foster biodiverse environments within dense urban settings.

Orchestrating Urban Flora and Fauna

Efficient urban biodiversity enhancement requires a symphony of efforts involving various players. City planners, ecologists, architects, and community members must harmonize their roles. Placing flora at the forefront, urban planting schemes should opt for flower-rich species, creating vibrant nectar and pollen sources. These attract pollinators essential for many plants' reproduction, ensuring dynamic ecosystems that sustain themselves and help perpetuate urban agriculture.

Encouraging urban wildlife requires more than crafting spaces; it also involves public education and engagement. Citizen science initiatives, where residents contribute to monitoring local biodiversity, can foster significant personal investment in maintaining these green urban sanctuaries. This participatory approach builds awareness and appreciation for biodiversity among city dwellers, fostering stewardship and encouraging wildlife-friendly practices.

Urban Biodiversity: A Historical Perspective

The concept of promoting biodiversity in urban environments has roots stretching back to the 19th-century garden cities movement championed by Ebenezer Howard. This movement, which sought to bring nature closer to urban living, laid the foundation for contemporary ecological urbanism. Historical precedence underscores the shift from managing nature as something external to integrating it within our cities, a strategy that remains vital today as urban areas expand globally.

Inspire to Preserve: Remarkable Results and Replication

A testament to successful urban biodiversity enhancement is found in the transformation of the once-gray city of Melbourne, Australia, into a sprawling green haven. By converting under-utilized spaces into wildlife-friendly environments and launching public initiatives like the City of Melbourne's Urban Forest Strategy, Melbourne has become a blueprint for cities worldwide seeking to replicate its flourishing biodiversity.

Similar initiatives across the globe, such as London's recent Urban Garden's initiative or Chicago's Green Roof program, demonstrate that cities, regardless of their unique challenges, can foster richer biodiversity. These projects serve as case studies and motivational blueprints, proving that biodiversity intervention can dramatically reshape urban landscapes.

The Future: Resilient Cities through Rich Biodiverse Tapestries

The future of urban landscapes lies in their ability to embrace biodiversity as an essential element of resilience. With the threat of climate change and urban expansion, the need for biodiverse cities is paramount. Future efforts may involve harnessing advancements in technology—like drone-aided tree planting and bio acoustic monitoring—to enhance urban ecological initiatives.

Political and societal advocacy for smaller, biodiverse interventions will continue to complement grand, citywide strategies. Balcony gardens or ultra-small parks may introduce critical "stepping stone" habitats essential for the survival of various species.

As urban planners and everyday citizens, recognizing and acting upon the potential to enrich biodiversity represents a fundamental, positive shift in how we perceive and interact with the cities that house us. This endeavor not only strengthens urban ecosystems but enriches our daily lives, ensuring we stay connected to the wonders of the natural world, no matter how city-bound we might find ourselves.

7.4   Urban Agriculture and Community Gardens

Amidst the skyline of concrete and steel, a verdant revolution is taking root. Urban agriculture and community gardens are transforming cities from gray expanses into tapestries of greens and hues, rich with the promise of food sustainability, community bonding, and environmental renewal. Growing produce isn't just for rural areas anymore; it's a thriving urban trend that saunters boldly into the heart of cities, bringing with it manifold benefits.

Farming the Concrete Jungle

Urban agriculture encapsulates the practice of cultivating, processing, and distributing food within and around urban zones. This can take numerous forms—from rooftop gardens and vertical farms to community plots and urban orchards. These initiatives not only supply fresh produce to urban residents but also contribute to a city's green infrastructure, which plays a pivotal role in enhancing local biodiversity and environmental sustainability.

City planners are increasingly recognizing the symbiotic relationship between urban land and agriculture, supporting initiatives that convert unused spaces, like vacant lots and rooftops, into productive green zones. Such transformations bring a dual benefit: mitigating the urban heat island effect and yielding fresh, local produce.

Fostering Food Security

One of the most lauded benefits of urban farming is its contribution to food security—a goal with ever-increasing importance as cities expand and global populations swell. Localized food production reduces dependence on rural agricultural systems, which are often distant, supply chain-dependent, and vulnerable to disruptions.

Urban farms make fresh fruits and vegetables available to communities where supermarkets might be scarce, thus helping to combat food deserts—regions with limited access to affordable and nutritious food. This is not only vital for nutritional health but also for economic equitability. Detroit, for instance, has seen vacant lots transformed into urban farms that provide local food sources to underserved communities, showcasing urban agriculture as a vital component of modern food systems.

Community Gardens: Building Bonds through Botany

If urban agriculture is the engine, community gardens are its heart—beating with social connectedness and co-operative spirit. These shared plots, often established in neighborhoods or city parks, serve as venues for collective gardening efforts, where individuals come together to plant, tend, and harvest.

Community gardens are more than just spaces for growing food; they are essential social infrastructures that foster connections. Whether it's an experienced gardener sharing wisdom with a novice, or neighbors working side by side to pull weeds, these interactions cultivate community solidarity and inclusivity. By engaging diverse groups in shared goals, community gardens have proven effective in bridging cultural and socioeconomic divides.

Educational opportunities abound in these green spaces. Many gardens host workshops and programs that teach sustainable farming, nutrition, and ecology to community members. Through hands-on participation, adults and children alike learn the intricacies of food production and the importance of sustainable practices—a grounding experience in an increasingly digital world.

Historical Roots and Modern Movements

Urban agriculture and community gardens are hardly a novel concept. Historically, they have seen varying prominence, notably during the World Wars when "victory gardens" proliferated to bolster domestic food supply. Yet, as cities urbanized post-war, these practices faded from the spotlight, supplanted by industrial agriculture.

In recent decades, however, they have witnessed a revival, driven by environmental awareness, health consciousness, and the desire for greater food sovereignty. Initiatives like Cuba's response to the collapse of Soviet support in the 1990s—with urban horticulture bolstering food resilience—exemplify the potential of these practices to bolster urban food systems.

Presently, cities like Vancouver and San Francisco are integrating urban agriculture into planning frameworks. These cities are pioneering policies and programs that incentivize local food production, granting tax benefits for properties that dedicate space to urban farming.

Cultivating Sustainability and Economic Opportunities

Urban agriculture simultaneously embraces and challenges modern economic paradigms. It embodies sustainability, reducing carbon footprints associated with food transport and packaging. Urban farms and gardens also introduce economic opportunities, particularly in peripheral areas, by generating employment through local produce markets, urban farming education, and agrotourism.

Moreover, while not a substitute for rural production, urban agriculture acts as a critical supplement. Technologies like hydroponics and aquaponics enable efficient food production within constrained urban settings, highlighting cities' potential to contribute meaningfully to local food supplies.

One inspiring example is the Devon Street Urban Farm in Chicago, which grows diverse crops using innovative vertical farming techniques. It not only addresses local food needs but also serves as a livelihood source, illustrating the multifaceted impact of urban agriculture.

Challenges and Opportunities for Growth

The embrace of urban agriculture is not without challenges. Regulatory barriers, land availability, and funding constraints often limit expansion. Yet innovative partnerships between municipalities, non-profits, and businesses offer pathways forward—such as leasing underutilized public lands for urban farming.

As climate change presses agricultural productivity and food systems globally, urban agriculture presents an opportunity—a chance to re-imagine cities as not just consumers, but also producers, of essential resources. Harnessing the interest and support of communities will be critical to scaling efforts and ensuring that urban agriculture thrives.

Greening the Future of Cities

Urban agriculture and community gardens offer more than palpable benefits; they ignite imaginations and inspire change. The greening of vacant lots and rooftops is a testament to the resilience and ingenuity of individuals striving to create a sustainable and equitable future. As cities continue to grow, the lessons learned from urban agriculture will be pivotal in ensuring cities remain livable, resilient, and richly connected to both nature and community.

7.5 Challenges in Maintaining Urban Greenery

Few would argue against the wisdom of threading green spaces through the urban fabric. However, realizing this vision is a journey rife with hurdles. Even as cities swell and concrete lays claim to once-verdant areas, the struggle to maintain and expand urban greenery persists. This section delves into the enduring obstacles that challenge our urban green ambitions.

Space: The Final Frontier

At the heart of the challenge lies a simple but daunting truth: cities are running out of space. With swelling populations driving the demand for housing, commercial spaces, and infrastructure, the quest for the remaining scraps of urban land is as fierce as in a game of Monopoly. Developers eye every vacant lot, while city planners are left to juggle priorities, often under fiscal constraints that leave little room for green dreams.

In these densely-packed areas, the calculus of converting land into green spaces versus residential or commercial developments often tilts in favor of concrete. While planners and environmental advocates work tirelessly to secure land for parks, their efforts can pale in comparison to the march of economic forces.

Funding and Budgetary Constraints

Green spaces, while relatively cost-effective long-term, do require initial investment and ongoing maintenance. For cash-strapped municipalities, the priority often rests on immediate fiscal needs such as infrastructure repairs, schools, or emergency services. The financial argument, often squeezed like a citrus fruit, leaves green projects a few drops short of funding.

This can lead to scenarios where projects stall or proceed without the necessary resources for their upkeep. When maintenance budgets run dry, parks degrade, equipment rusts, and greenery withers, ultimately turning public enthusiasm into disenchantment.

Governance and Policy Hiccups

A maze of policy and governance issues constructs yet another barrier to urban greenery. The challenge is not merely the presence of policy but its lag behind urban realities. Often, the regulatory environment poses restrictions or lacks incentives that could foster green space creation or maintenance.

Fragmented authority, where responsibilities for green spaces are divided among different agencies, can lead to inefficiencies. Effective urban greenery initiatives require coordination and collaboration across government departments, private sectors, and community groups. However, bureaucratic inertia often stifles potential cooperative efforts, paving a pathway fraught with roadblocks rather than flowering avenues.

Environmental Stressors

Urban green spaces are not just ornamental additions; they function as vital, living components of city ecosystems. As such, they face numerous environmental stressors that challenge their vitality. Pollution, both airborne and soil-bound, can degrade plant health, attenuate biodiversity, and necessitate constant remediation efforts.

Cities also amplify the impacts of climate change, presenting unique hurdles to the sustainability of urban greenery. Variability in weather conditions—longer heatwaves, unexpected frosts, or intense storms—can devastate urban plant life that is already in a delicate balance. This scenario requires evolving strategies in plant selection and care to keep pace with the changing climate.

Public Engagement and Participation

While green spaces evoke public approval, ensuring ongoing engagement is a complex dance. Participation declines when communities do not see themselves as stakeholders in maintaining these spaces or if they perceive them as poorly maintained and unsafe.

Fostering a culture where everyone is a steward of public green spaces involves more than just outreach; it requires grassroots involvement and education, enabling communities to connect with nature and take pride in its preservation. Community gardens and volunteering opportunities can rally the public to appreciate and defend urban green spaces, engendering shared responsibility rather than dependence on municipal bodies alone.

Innovative Solutions to Thrive

Despite these daunting challenges, innovation is the prevailing wind that can redirect the course of urban greenery. Innovative land use policies can incentivize the integration of more green spaces within urban developments. Some cities adopt green roofs or vertical gardens as part of urban building codes, marrying development with greenery.

Partnerships between cities and private enterprises can generate funding, with industries often eager to align themselves with environmental sustainability. Sponsored parks or collaborative urban farming initiatives illustrate how public-private ventures can overcome budgetary limitations.

Urban residents increasingly turning to digital platforms for engagement delivers another opportunity. Apps for public reporting on the state of local parks or initiatives gamifying volunteerism in green space maintenance are promising tools to enhance public participation.

Learning from Leaders

Cities like Curitiba in Brazil have set a precedent with their holistic urban planning that places greenery at the heart of development. Renowned for its pedestrian-friendly streets and vast green areas, it serves as a model of integrating sustainability while mitigating economic and spatial constraints.

Similarly, Copenhagen's commitment to becoming

131

carbon-neutral is underscored by its expansive green network, designed as a critical infrastructure that supports ecological well-being and fosters a better urban habitat.

Cultivating the Urban Future

Maintaining and expanding urban green spaces embodies the arduous yet rewarding effort of steering cities toward a sustainable future. Overcoming challenges requires recognizing green spaces as essential urban infrastructure rather than ancillary amenities.

By navigating the complex web of policy, finance, and community involvement, cities can reap the benefits of urban greenery—a tapestry woven with resilience, vitality, and beauty that enhances both ecological health and human well-being. As we push into the future, nurturing our urban landscapes will continue to define the success stories of our cities' growth and transformation.

Chapter 8

Social Equity and Community Engagement

This chapter examines the role of social equity in sustainable urban development, identifying barriers to equitable planning. It outlines strategies for inclusive community engagement and the significance of public spaces in fostering social integration. Highlighting successful cases of community empowerment, it emphasizes that equitable, engaged urban communities are vital for achieving sustainability, enhancing resident well-being, and addressing systemic challenges collaboratively.

8.1 Understanding Social Equity in Urban Contexts

Social equity is a pivotal component in the quest for sustainable urban development, serving as the ethical heart that guides the growth of our cities. To truly grasp this concept, imagine a city where every resident, regardless of their socioeconomic status, ethnicity, age, or ability, has access to the same opportunities and resources. This ideal may seem lofty, but it's an essential ambition if we are to develop cities that are not just economically viable and environmentally sound, but also socially just. As urban areas burgeon, accommodating a majority of the world's population, the quest for social equity becomes not only a moral obligation but a practical necessity in creating resilient, thriving communities.

Historically, cities have been the engines of economic growth and innovation, offering countless possibilities to their inhabitants. However, they have also been landscapes of stark inequalities. The industrial revolution, while propelling unprecedented urban expansion and economic opportunity, also accentuated divides, with burgeoning factories and vast wealth coexisting alongside pervasive poverty and squalor. These historical patterns have laid the groundwork for the present-day urban disparities we see today, where access to quality education, healthcare, housing, and employment continues to be unequally distributed.

The concept of social equity in urban planning emerged in response to these disparities, advocating for a design of urban policies and spaces that foster inclusivity and access for all citizens. This manifests in various domains, from transportation systems that connect peripheral neighborhoods to economic hubs, to affordable housing initiatives aimed at preventing displacement due to gentrification. Social equity in urban contexts thus acts as a multifaceted remedy, seeking to balance the scales of opportunity and enrich the lived experiences of all city dwellers.

A pertinent example can be found in the sphere of housing. In many global cities, housing has become a commodity subject to market whims, often leading to skyrocketing prices and the marginalization of less affluent populations. To counter this, some cities have embraced inclusive zoning policies, which require new developments to offer a certain percentage of units at below-market rates. These policies aim to integrate lower-income families into thriving neighborhoods, ensuring that access to good schools, healthy environments, and job opportunities are not exclusive privileges.

Social equity also finds its expression in urban transport networks. Consider the implementation of subsidized public transit fares, which remove one of the barriers that prevent low-income individuals from accessing employment opportunities across the city. By improving the mobility of all citizens, we ensure that economic participation is not geographically restricted. Moreover, equitable transit planning involves designing routes that not only serve the economically prosperous areas but also penetrate underserved neighborhoods, thus stitching together the urban fabric in more cohesive and inclusive ways.

Yet, addressing social equity isn't solely about the physical modifications of urban spaces; it's also about the processes through which these spaces are developed. Meaningful community engagement is crucial. Cities that engage with their communities through participatory planning processes are more likely to create environments that reflect the diverse voices and needs of their inhabitants. This involves more than just token consultation; it's about cultivating genuine dialogue and fostering partnerships with community members who have historically been excluded from decision-making processes.

A successful example can be found in Medellín, Colombia, where citizen involvement was central to the city's transformation from a place historically plagued by violence and social inequity to a model of innovative urban development. The city's approach was holistic, incorporating physical upgrades like the construction of public libraries and parks in underserved districts, combined with a concerted effort to include residents in the planning process. This partnership between the government and its people has not only improved living conditions but has also strengthened the social fabric of the city, fostering a sense of shared ownership and responsibility.

From these examples, it's clear that addressing social equity in urban contexts involves not only policies and planning but also a cultural shift toward collective discernment and action. Urban environments enriched by social equity contribute to more harmonious social dynamics, diminish conflict, and enhance overall well-being. By acknowledging and addressing disparities, cities can craft environments that sustain not only the economic and environmental pillars of their futures but also the social.

Social equity represents more than an abstract ideal; it is a practical strategy for building urban landscapes that are inclusive, sustainable, and vibrant. As we continue to witness the rapid evolution of our cities, integrating social equity into urban planning becomes imperative. By doing so, we can create urban spaces where diversity is not just accommodated but celebrated, and where opportunity and prosperity are shared across all facets of society. Only then can we consider our cities truly sustainable in all senses of the word.

8.2   Barriers to Equitable Urban Planning

Urban planning aims to shape the environments in which we live, but achieving social equity in this endeavor is easier said than done. As cities juggle rapid urbanization, economic pressures, and diverse populations, several formidable barriers stand in the way of ensuring that no resident is left behind. Understanding these challenges is crucial for dismantling them and paving the way for more inclusive urban growth.

One of the primary barriers to equitable urban planning is the persistence of historical inequities. Many cities carry the legacy of past policies that favored certain groups over others, leading to entrenched disparities. Redlining practices in the United States, for example, systematically denied mortgages to Black families in certain neighborhoods, preventing wealth accumulation and access to quality housing and education. These historical dynamics have contemporary echoes, creating disparities that persist despite intentions to reform.

Furthermore, urban planners often grapple with the challenge of limited financial resources and competing priorities. Public budgets rarely match the scale of the social challenges cities face, forcing difficult decisions regarding which projects to fund. Investments tend to favor areas that promise quick economic returns, often leaving behind neighborhoods that are more in need of development. The tension between economic viability and social equity can result in a status quo where marginalized communities are neglected.

Political dynamics also play a crucial role. Urban policy-making is inherently political, and power imbalances can skew planning agendas. Decision-making bodies often include some demographics and interests over others, sidelining the needs of underrepresented communities. Lobbying and political influence can disproportionately shape urban policy, leading to developments that favor commercial interests over those of current residents, particularly in vulnerable communities.

Gentrification, a term that captures the transformative

revaluation of urban areas, often raises eyebrows in discussions on urban equity. While the modernization and revitalization of urban areas can bring new amenities and raise property values, they also risk displacing long-standing residents.   The cultural and social displacement of communities, as the cost of living surges, results in a loss of social capital, where longtime residents find themselves priced out of the neighborhoods they call home.   Solutions to prevent gentrification-related displacement, such as implementing community land trusts or regulating rental markets, face numerous technical and political hurdles.

In addition, there are structural siloes within governmental and planning agencies that impede cohesive planning.   Departmental fragmentation means that initiatives in housing, transportation, education, and health services are often developed in isolation from one another. Such compartmentalization results in projects that are narrow in scope and lacking in comprehensive vision. An integrated approach that coordinates across departments and considers the multifaceted nature of social equity is crucial but often lacking due to bureaucratic inertia.

Moreover, the rapid pace of technological change presents both opportunities and barriers to equitable urban planning.   While smart city technologies offer the chance to make cities more livable and efficient, they also risk excluding those without access to digital infrastructure.   Urban planners must confront the "digital divide"—the gap between those who have easy access to computers and the internet, and those who do not. Bridging this divide is essential for ensuring that all city residents can participate in the benefits of smart urban development.

Lastly, public engagement processes, which are intended to democratize planning and bring in diverse voices, often fall short. Tokenistic consultations, where community input is solicited but not meaningfully integrated into final decisions, can exacerbate feelings of exclusion and mistrust among residents. Ensuring genuine participation in urban planning requires not only inviting community voices but empowering them to influence outcomes and fostering continuous dialogue.

Practical examples illustrate both the challenges and possibilities for overcoming these barriers. Consider the city of Curitiba in Brazil, which faced rapid growth and resource constraints in the late 20th century. Rather than succumb to chaos, Curitiba implemented integrated urban planning solutions that focused on public transportation, affordable housing, and green space, becoming a model for other cities. Success stories like Curitiba emphasize that barriers are not insurmountable; they require innovative solutions and political will.

While the barriers to equitable urban planning are numerous and complex, recognizing them is the first step toward overcoming them. Whether dealing with historical injustices, navigating political landscapes, or fostering genuine community engagement, cities have a mandate to ensure that development serves all citizens. By approaching urban planning with determination, empathy, and inclusivity, planners can help fashion cities that are not only successful but equitable, laying the foundations for sustainable urban development.

8.3 Strategies for Inclusive Community Engagement

Inclusive community engagement forms the backbone of successful urban planning. Yet, engaging diverse communities requires more than just ticking off a checklist. It is about ensuring representation, empowering voices, and fostering an ongoing dialogue that evolves with the community's needs. It may sound like a daunting task, yet when done right, the rewards include enriched social cohesion, better project outcomes, and cities that reflect the desires and aspirations of all their inhabitants.

To embark on this journey, one must first understand the diverse tapestry of urban communities. Cities are melting pots of cultures, languages, and backgrounds, making the concept of "community" multidimensional. Effective engagement recognizes this diversity and aims to create platforms where every voice not only speaks but is heard—starting with establishing trust, a crucial first step often overlooked in traditional planning processes. Trust-building can take many forms, from informal gatherings to regular community feedback sessions where city planners listen more than they talk.

A historical lens offers insight into why trust must be established. For decades, many communities have been burnt by empty promises and plans that steamrolled local needs in favor of broader aims. This historical baggage means urban planners need to approach engagement with transparency, acknowledging previous missteps and committing to a democratic process where the community has a genuine stake in decisions. Acknowledging history can lead to healing and open the doors to genuine collaboration.

But how do we bring communities into the fold in a

140

meaningful way? Participatory planning is key. Rooted in the idea that those who are affected by plans should have a hand in making them, this approach moves beyond consultation to co-creation. One successful model is the use of charrettes, intensive planning sessions where community members, planners, and designers collaborate to develop visions for urban spaces. These sessions are dynamic, often producing innovative solutions that may not emerge in traditional, more top-down planning methods.

Moreover, modern technology offers untapped potential to enhance participatory approaches. Digital platforms can democratize the planning process by making information more accessible and inviting broader participation. Online surveys, virtual reality simulations of proposed developments, and interactive mapping tools allow community members to visualize and understand potential changes to their urban environment. Nevertheless, this approach must be sensitive to the digital divide, ensuring technology complements rather than supplants traditional engagement methods.

The living example of Porto Alegre, Brazil, illustrates the transformative power of inclusive engagement. The city's participatory budgeting process invites citizens to decide how to allocate parts of the municipal budget. Porto Alegre's model has thrived due to its consistency and transparency, with citizens directly reacting to budgetary proposals and tracking their implementation over time. This model has not only empowered citizens but also enhanced governmental accountability.

Effective engagement also means dismantling barriers that prevent participation. Language access is crucial; providing materials and conducting meetings in multiple languages accommodates non-native speakers, ensuring language is not a barrier to

141

participation. Childcare and transportation are other key components—offering them at meetings can enable those with constraints to attend and engage.

Inclusion means reaching out to and empowering those oft-silenced or underrepresented, such as minority communities, young people, and the elderly. For example, youth-focused engagement initiatives can utilize social media platforms, which serve as natural mediums for younger demographics. By integrating youth voices into urban planning, cities can tap into fresh perspectives and innovations while fostering a generation that feels both valued and invested in their community's future.

Lastly, the design and facilitation of engagement activities can greatly influence outcomes. Moving away from sterile city hall meetings to more contextually relevant locations—community centers, local parks, or even pop-up events in the middle of the community—can make the process feel more accessible. Activities that are interactive and participatory, such as workshops that include games or simulations, often yield richer engagement than formal presentations or public hearings.

Inclusive community engagement is far more than a checkbox in urban planning—it is an ethos that, when embraced, can revolutionize the way cities develop and function. By ensuring all voices are acknowledged and empowered in the urban planning process, cities not only become more equitable but also more innovative, as diverse perspectives spur creative solutions to shared challenges. The journey toward inclusive engagement is ongoing, but with commitment and creativity, cities can become true reflections of the people who inhabit them.

8.4 Role of Public Spaces in Social Integration

Public spaces hold a unique power in urban environments: they are the great social levellers and integration engines of our cities. As neutral ground accessible to everyone, parks, plazas, streets, and community centers can weave the diverse threads of society into a cohesive social fabric. Understanding how public spaces contribute to social integration requires exploring the physical environments they create and the social interactions they nurture.

Historically, public spaces have served as focal points of civic life, from the agoras of ancient Greece that fueled democratic participation to the vibrant town squares in medieval Europe that hosted markets and festivals. These spaces fostered social interaction and idea exchange, creating a shared communal life that was crucial for societal cohesion. Today, as cities become more complex mosaics of different cultures and backgrounds, the role of public spaces in promoting social integration is more crucial than ever.

The physical design of public spaces can either encourage or inhibit social interaction. Consider New York's Central Park. It was envisioned by Frederick Law Olmsted and Calvert Vaux in the mid-19th century as a democratic refuge where city dwellers from all walks of life could mingle, relax, and reconnect with nature. Its pathways, open meadows, and clutches of trees facilitate easy movement and spontaneous social encounters, inviting people to interact naturally. Such considered design elements are vital in crafting spaces that are welcoming to diverse community members.

Moreover, well-designed public spaces can bridge

143

divides by providing common ground in the most literal
sense. Streetscapes equipped with wide sidewalks,
benches, and pedestrian-friendly crossroads invite
leisurely strolls and impromptu conversations. Plazas
with movable seating and ample shade encourage
lengthy stays, making them attractive meeting spots
across differing weather conditions. These spaces often
become backdrops to our daily lives, offering settings
for interactions, from friendly nods between strangers
to lively public debates.

Community gardens are another excellent example.
They transform overlooked urban spaces into green
oases where residents cultivate plants and relationships
simultaneously. Such gardens bring neighbors from
varying backgrounds together, uniting them with
a shared purpose of nurturing their community.
In addition, community gardens host events and
workshops, further integrating seasonal activities with
opportunities for learning and collaboration.

Inclusion is not just about spatial design but also about
intentional programming. Public events like outdoor
concerts, food festivals, and arts and crafts fairs animate
public spaces in ways that transcend cultural barriers.
For example, street festivals celebrating a particular
cultural heritage can transform a neighborhood street
into a canvas of multicultural engagement, attracting
crowds of all demographics. Through these public
gatherings, communities forge connections that enrich
their social tapestry.

Public spaces also facilitate intergenerational interaction, essential for truly inclusive social integration.
Playgrounds designed with both children's play
and adult relaxation in mind, spaces like the Parc
de la Villette in Paris, offer engaging environments
for families. Meanwhile, integrating game tables or

144

exercise stations into park designs encourages older adults to frequent these areas, naturally fostering multi-generational interaction.

Consider the city of Medellin, Colombia, which has purposefully harnessed the transformative potential of public space in social integration. Once known for its social and economic disparities, the city has revitalized neighborhoods through urban acupuncture, which strategically creates small but impactful points of intervention, such as public libraries with attached parks in underserved areas. These spaces not only provide educational resources but also become communal hubs where people from different backgrounds or neighborhoods meet.

Yet, there are challenges to ensuring that public spaces achieve their potential for social integration. Issues of accessibility and maintenance can hinder their full use. For instance, infrastructure such as ramps for wheelchairs, sufficient lighting for safety, and public transit connections ensures that everyone—not just the able-bodied or the affluent—can enjoy these communal resources. Regular maintenance ensures that these spaces remain inviting and safe, free from the blight that neglect can bring.

Moreover, meaningful community involvement in the design and management of public spaces can enhance their integrative role. Initiatives like the grassroots-driven placemaking movement emphasize local knowledge in shaping environments that are genuinely attuned to community needs. This empowerment can turn public spaces into stages for social innovation and resilience, as local communities invent unique, home-grown solutions to urban challenges.

Public spaces are not just amenities in our urban landscapes—they are critical arenas for fostering social

145

integration.   When effectively designed and utilized,
they can transform cities into inclusive environments
where all residents feel a sense of belonging. By inviting
interaction, bridging cultural gaps, and encouraging
community participation, public spaces build the social
cohesion that is vital for thriving urban civilization.
Through thoughtful design and vibrant programming,
cities can harness the power of public spaces to ensure
that they become vibrant beacons of unity in an
increasingly diverse world.

8.5   Case Studies of Successful Community Empowerment

Community empowerment is the secret ingredient that
transforms neighborhoods from places on a map to vibrant, thriving centers of life. It shifts the narrative from
passive governance to active citizen participation, where
communities no longer wait for top-down policies but instead wield the power to shape their environments. Let's
explore several compelling case studies from around the
globe that illuminate the path to successful community
empowerment, enhancing social equity and invigorating
civic life.

Our first stop is Seoul, South Korea, where the city
government has been actively engaging its citizens
through the "Seoul 2030 Plan." Realizing that urban
development needed more than a bureaucratic touch,
city officials invited citizens to participate in shaping
the future of their urban environment.   The plan
involved setting up several citizen committees and
introducing participatory budgeting, where citizens
could propose and vote on local projects. This inclusive
approach not only empowered residents by giving them
a voice in financial decision-making but also promoted

transparency and accountability within the government. The result? Increased trust between citizens and the government, leading to urban projects that truly reflect the public's priorities and needs.

Across the Atlantic, in London, the story of the Coin Street Community Builders (CSCB) exemplifies grass-roots perseverance in the face of adversity. In the early 1980s, the South Bank area was slated for commercial development, which threatened to displace local residents. A coalition of local citizens banded together to purchase the land through innovative community funding and transform it into cooperative housing and public space. Today, CSCB has successfully developed affordable housing and community amenities that emphasize cooperative ownership, securing long-term affordability and fostering a close-knit community. This initiative demonstrates that with determination and strategic action, communities can reclaim the right to their city.

Moving to South America, we find another inspiring tale of community empowerment in Porto Alegre, Brazil—a city already mentioned for its pioneering participatory budgeting. Here, each year, thousands of citizens congregate to discuss and decide on public spending priorities. What's remarkable is the level of grassroots engagement and turnout, with citizens from all walks of life—including marginalized groups—actively participating. This process not only democratizes budget allocation but also educates citizens about civic processes, creating a more informed and politically engaged populace. The Porto Alegre model has inspired other cities worldwide, proving that grassroots democratic processes can flourish even in large urban centers.

Community empowerment is also thriving in Africa, particularly in the Kibera slum of Nairobi, Kenya—

147

often cited as one of the largest informal settlements
in Africa. A community-led initiative known as the
"Shining Hope for Communities" (SHOFCO) has been
pivotal in transforming the area. Beginning with the
belief that community empowerment is driven by
local solutions, SHOFCO initiated projects focused on
health, education, and gender equity. Among their
successes is the Kibera School for Girls—a free school
providing education and meals to the community's
most vulnerable members.   SHOFCO's endeavors
demonstrate the power of focusing on local needs and
resources to impart lasting socio-economic change.

In the United States, the Dudley Street Neighborhood
Initiative (DSNI) in Boston illustrates an empowering
community ownership story. Faced with disinvestment
in the late 20th century, the neighborhood experienced
widespread neglect and decay. In response, residents
mobilized to form DSNI, gaining the rare power of em-
inent domain over vacant land. This authority enabled
them to negotiate community-driven redevelopment, resulting in affordable housing and communal spaces tailored to the residents' specifications. DSNI's success not
only benefited its immediate neighborhood but also inspired policy changes in community land trust practices
across the country.

Finally, let's consider Medellín, Colombia, where,
beyond the improvements to public spaces and
transportation, as previously highlighted, the city's
Comprehensive Urban Project (Proyecto Urbano
Integral, PUI) serves as another benchmark of
community empowerment.   The PUI was designed
to integrate marginalized areas with the rest of the city
through participatory planning processes. Community
members were deeply involved in the design and
implementation stages, ensuring projects catered to local

needs. Not only did this foster a sense of ownership and pride, but it also dismantled socioeconomic barriers, reimagining Medellín as a city of cooperation and shared progress.

These varied case studies underscore that community empowerment is not one-size-fits-all but a diverse operation reflective of local contexts and needs. Across continents and cultures, these initiatives share common values of trust, participation, and shared responsibility. They emphasize the potential for ordinary citizens to affect extraordinary change, proving that empowered communities can indeed reclaim agency over their urban futures.

By learning from these successes, cities around the world can cultivate environments where community empowerment isn't just possible—it's inevitable. These initiatives are beacons illuminating the path for other communities seeking to assert their rights, build their capacity, and create equitable urban spaces that cater to the diverse rhythms of the 21st-century city.

CHAPTER 8.   SOCIAL EQUITY AND COMMUNITY ENGAGEMENT

Chapter 9

Technology and Innovation in Sustainable Cities

This chapter explores the transformative impact of smart technologies in enhancing urban sustainability. It delves into innovative infrastructure solutions, data-driven urban management, and the applications of AI and IoT. Addressing challenges and ethical considerations, it emphasizes how technology facilitates efficient resource use and improved city services, empowering cities to meet sustainability goals while enhancing urban living quality.

9.1 Smart City Technologies

In the mosaic of urban landscapes, a new paradigm is emerging—cities transformed by the integration of smart technologies. These are not just products of science fiction fantasies, but tangible innovations that promise to dramatically alter the way cities operate. At the heart of this transformation lies a symphony of sensors, data analytics, and connectivity that collectively aim to craft more sustainable and efficient urban environments.

Technology, in this context, becomes an urban artisan,

151

shaping the intricate tapestry of city life. But what makes a city 'smart'? Imagine streetlights that dim or brighten based on pedestrian activity and weather conditions, or waste bins that signal sanitation workers when they're full. Consider noise sensors that alert city officials to breaches in acceptable noise levels, thereby enhancing community well-being. These examples illustrate a fraction of the possibilities, yet highlight a core theme: the smart city is one that leverages technology to respond intelligently to the needs of its inhabitants.

The Anatomy of Smart Cities

At a fundamental level, smart cities rely on a delicate interplay of infrastructure and digital technology. Sensors, the silent observers, gather data from myriad aspects of city life—from traffic flows to energy consumption patterns. This data is then processed by advanced software systems that identify patterns, predict potential issues, and suggest optimized solutions. For instance, in Stockholm, sensors embedded in the city's water management system provide real-time data to predict rainfall and control stormwater, reducing the risk of flooding.

Underpinning these systems is a robust framework of connectivity. The Internet of Things (IoT) acts as the neural network of a smart city, linking disparate systems to create a cohesive whole. In Barcelona, a pioneer in smart city initiatives, IoT-enabled lampposts provide Wi-Fi, environmental monitoring, and guide vehicles to available parking spots. The integration of such technologies is not merely about convenience; it's about reshaping urban living to be more efficient and sustainable.

Historical Roots and Progress

The notion of a smart city isn't entirely a product of recent technological advancements. Its roots can be traced back to the city of Songdo in South Korea, often touted as the world's first smart city. Conceived in the early 2000s, Songdo was built from scratch with an integrated smart grid, waste disposal systems, and efficient public transport networks. Though initially seen as an ambitious experiment, it set a precedent, illustrating that urban efficiency and environmental responsibility could go hand-in-hand.

As the years progressed, the idea of smart cities found its way into existing metropolises. Cities like Amsterdam embraced open data initiatives, allowing entrepreneurs and developers to create apps that further improve city life—from energy-saving tools to platforms that bolster local businesses. These efforts align with the key principle that smart cities aren't just tech marvels—they are fundamentally people-centric environments.

Environmental Sustainability and Efficiency

Arguably, the most compelling aspect of smart city technologies is their potential to catalyze environmental sustainability. Urban areas, with their towering buildings and bustling streets, are significant contributors to global carbon emissions. Yet, by optimizing how energy and resources are consumed, smart technologies can dramatically lessen this impact.

Consider the concept of 'smart grids,' which enable more efficient electricity distribution by dynamically responding to demand and incorporating renewable energy sources. Copenhagen's smart grid system uses data to ensure that energy produced by wind turbines is effectively utilized, reducing reliance on fossil fuels.

Moreover, the mobility sector stands to benefit immensely from smart innovations. Public transportation systems, enhanced by real-time data, can dramatically improve efficiency, cutting down both wait times for

153

passengers and idle times for vehicles.   Singapore's intelligent transport system monitors traffic congestion, adjusting traffic light sequences dynamically, which not only eases congestion but also reduces vehicular emissions.

Citizen-Centric Approaches

While technology forms the backbone of smart cities, its true success hinges on the engagement of its inhabitants. A smart city must cater not only to efficiency but also to the empowerment of its citizens, offering them tools to participate in decision-making processes. Crowdsourcing platforms, for instance, allow residents to report issues in their neighborhoods, from potholes to streetlight outages.   New York City's "311" app exemplifies this approach, enabling citizens to actively contribute to the city's maintenance and improvement.

Furthermore, educational initiatives are pivotal in ensuring that citizens can effectively interact with new technologies. Workshops, training sessions, and online resources must be part of the smart city agenda to close any digital divide and allow the benefits of smart technologies to permeate through all societal layers.

Challenges and Ethical Considerations

Deploying smart technologies is not without its challenges. Data privacy concerns loom large as cities gather vast amounts of information.   It is essential to establish transparent governance frameworks that safeguard citizens' privacy while enabling data-driven innovation.

Equally important is addressing the risk of technological disparity. As smart cities evolve, ensuring equitable access to technological benefits remains a critical concern. Strategies that promote inclusivity are paramount, ensuring that all citizens enjoy the fruits of these advancements, not just a privileged few.

Smart city technologies present a fascinating frontier in urban development. By aligning technological innovation with human-centric urban planning, these technologies offer a pathway to sustainable and efficient cities. While challenges exist, they serve as opportunities to cultivate environments that not only thrive economically and ecologically but also empower citizens to become active stewards of their communities. This balance is the quintessence of a truly smart city—one that marries ingenuity with sustainability, technology with humanity.

9.2 Innovative Infrastructure Solutions

In the quest for more sustainable and vibrant urban environments, innovative infrastructure solutions have emerged as keystones. These contemporary feats of engineering and urban planning are reshaping the fabric of our cities, pushing the boundaries of efficiency, resilience, and ecological consciousness. Like masterful sculptures in the landscape of urban advancement, they reflect our aspirations to blend functionality with sustainability.

Historically, the development of cities was synonymous with massive infrastructures—roads, bridges, sewage systems—the skeletal framework upon which urban life was built. However, this conventional infrastructure, with its carbon-heavy footprint and voracious resource appetite, is increasingly seen as unsustainable. Enter, stage right, the new wave of infrastructure innovation: dynamic, adaptable, and conscious of its surrounding environment.

The Emergence of Green Infrastructure

At the forefront of these innovations stands green infrastructure. No longer a mere novelty, it has become pivotal in addressing urban environmental challenges. Unlike the rigid, gray infrastructure of old, green infrastructure introduces a new dimension by harmoniously integrating nature into urban settings. Consider New York City's High Line, a defunct elevated railway repurposed into a linear park, offering urban green space and biodiversity corridors amidst the concrete jungle.

Such projects are not merely aesthetic but practical. They serve as urban lungs, reducing heat and improving air quality while simultaneously managing stormwater. Rain gardens, green roofs, and permeable pavements actively reduce runoff, alleviating strain on traditional drainage systems. The underlying philosophy is simple: work with nature, not against it.

Modular and Adaptive Infrastructure

The unpredictability of climate change necessitates infrastructure that can adapt as conditions evolve. Enter modular and adaptive infrastructures—designed with flexibility and resilience at their core. These systems can be incrementally expanded or adapted without the need for extensive resources or time. In rapidly growing cities, such as those in developing countries, this approach enables infrastructure to scale with population demands.

Take for instance the modular floating structures in the Netherlands, developed in response to rising sea levels. These floating neighborhoods, marvels of adaptive design, allow communities to thrive even as water encroaches. Similarly, in Tokyo, modular flood barriers are deployed along flood-prone areas, capable of extension or retraction as necessary, showcasing the elegance of adaptable solutions in safeguarding urban areas.

Intelligent Transport Infrastructure

With urban populations steadily increasing, cities face relentless pressure to provide efficient and sustainable transport solutions. Enter intelligent transport infrastructures—sophisticated networks that synchronize transport operations to minimize congestion and emissions. Unlike traditional systems, these innovations leverage real-time data and predictive algorithms to optimize route planning, traffic light sequencing, and public transit schedules.

Consider London's Crossrail, a mammoth project blending cutting-edge engineering with subterranean tunneling to expand the city's rail capacity. While impressive, the true marvel lies in its accompanying integrated communication systems, which dynamically adjust train movements and passenger flows in response to real-time data. Similarly, in cities like Helsinki, open data initiatives offer citizens seamless, multimodal travel options, reducing reliance on personal vehicles and their associated emissions.

Digital Twins and Infrastructure Monitoring

To bolster infrastructural resilience, cities are now turning to 'digital twins'—virtual models that mirror physical infrastructure. These digital representations allow planners and engineers to simulate conditions, predict failure points, and test potential upgrades without any physical disruption.

Singapore has been a vanguard in this area, developing a comprehensive digital twin of the city. This virtual model facilitates a proactive approach to infrastructure maintenance and disaster management, from predicting floods due to overburdened drainage systems to optimizing energy use in public buildings. Such technology not only enhances efficiency but also extends the lifespan and functionality of infrastructure, yielding significant sustainability benefits.

Energy-Optimized Infrastructure

A significant proportion of urban emissions arises from the demand for energy to power infrastructure. Therefore, forward-thinking cities are embedding energy optimization into the very blueprints of their urban designs. Smart grids, once again playing a crucial role, now connect not only homes and businesses but also urban infrastructure.

Infrastructure projects, such as the Hudson Yards development in New York City, exemplify this integration. By embedding advanced energy systems, such as cogeneration plants that convert waste heat into electricity, and intelligent building designs that adjust dynamically to occupancy and weather, these projects minimize energy consumption while optimizing performance.

Elsewhere, cities like Copenhagen are harnessing district heating systems, utilizing heat from industrial processes, and redistributing it to nearby buildings. This is a remarkable step toward decoupling urban infrastructure development from fossil fuel dependency, mitigating climate change impacts and promoting sustainability.

The innovative infrastructure solutions painting the canvas of modern cities are not free from challenge. They require substantial investment, robust policy frameworks, and a cultural shift toward valuing sustainability. Yet, as these case studies demonstrate, the benefits far outweigh the costs. These infrastructures not only animate cities with vitality and efficiency, but they also become living testaments to human ingenuity.

As the world accelerates toward an urban future, embracing these infrastructure innovations is not just beneficial—it's imperative. These solutions, resplendent in their marriage of technology and nature, offer a glimmering promise, illuminating a path toward a more sustainable and resilient urban tomorrow. They remind us that cities are not static constructs, but ever-evolving ecosystems capable of innovation and adaptation, if only we dare to reshape them accordingly.

9.3 Data-Driven Urban Management

Imagine a city that runs as seamlessly as a finely-tuned orchestra, harmonizing the everyday complexities of urban life through the subtle yet profound influence of data. Welcome to the world of data-driven urban management, where bits and bytes become the unsung heroes of city spaces, transforming the chaos of urban environments into symphonic efficiency.

At its core, data-driven urban management involves harnessing vast amounts of data to optimize city operations and enhance public services. This endeavor not only improves the quality of life for citizens but does so with a respect for environmental sustainability and economic sensibility. As we delve into this topic, it becomes evident that data is not merely supplementary but fundamental to the future of urban governance.

The Data Renaissance in Urban Settings

The notion of employing data to manage cities isn't entirely new. Historically, cities have utilized data in various forms, from census information to traffic

159

counts, to inform planning and services. However, the contemporary data renaissance is characterized by an unprecedented volume, velocity, and variety of data, driven largely by the advent of digital technology and the Internet of Things (IoT). This explosion of data presents new opportunities for insights that were previously unimaginable.

Cities such as Chicago have leveraged this digital momentum by developing robust data analytics platforms. The Windy City's "Array of Things" project epitomizes this ambition, with sensors perched atop streetlights collecting data on air quality, noise, and temperature, revealing detailed snapshots of urban life. These insights are not lost in dusty archives but are actively employed to address urban challenges.

The Art of Data Analytics in Urban Management

Transforming raw data into actionable intelligence requires sophisticated analytics systems, akin to turning raw ingredients into a gourmet meal. Techniques such as predictive analytics and machine learning discern patterns and forecast future scenarios with remarkable accuracy. This is particularly beneficial for optimizing city operations like public transport scheduling, waste management, and emergency services.

Take, for example, Los Angeles' use of predictive policing, where historical crime data is combined with real-time analytics to deploy law enforcement resources more effectively. This data-driven approach not only enhances public safety but does so efficiently, directing attention and resources where they are needed most.

Enhancing Public Services through Data

The power of data extends far beyond law enforcement.

Consider public health, where data analytics streamline the early detection and response to outbreaks. The COVID-19 pandemic highlighted the essential role of data in public health strategy, as cities around the globe, such as London, utilized real-time data to track infection rates and optimize healthcare resource allocation.

Similarly, in education, data-driven management systems have revolutionized how resources are allocated to schools. By analyzing performance metrics and demographic data, cities can ensure equitable distribution of educational resources, attending to underserved areas and identifying best practices through data-backed insights.

Traffic and Transportation: A Data-Driven Revolution

A perennial bane of city living, traffic congestion can be effectively tackled through data-driven approaches. Urban areas, from Tokyo to Toronto, employ real-time data to enhance traffic flow, adjusting traffic signals dynamically based on current conditions, and providing commuters with up-to-date travel information.

In public transportation, data analytics optimize bus routes and schedules. By analyzing passenger data and predictive models, transit agencies can ensure buses and trains are efficient and responsive to demand, reducing wait times and emissions alike. When Barcelona embraced such methodologies, they saw marked improvements in public transport efficiency and user satisfaction.

Data Governance: A Necessity for Trust and Transparency

While data-driven urban management holds great promise, it is not without its challenges. Chief among these is the issue of data governance—ensuring data is handled responsibly, ethically, and transparently. Without proper data protection measures and policies, the very foundation of trust can crumble, deterring citizen engagement and cooperation.

To this end, cities like Toronto have pioneered open data initiatives, making non-sensitive data publicly accessible to encourage innovation while respecting privacy concerns. These platforms invite academia, businesses, and citizens to contribute to city problem-solving, democratizing the decision-making process and fostering an empowered community.

Building Resilience through Data

Finally, one of the most compelling applications of data-driven urban management is in building urban resilience. In an era marked by climate change, natural disasters, and rapid urbanization, the ability to quickly respond to and recover from disruptions is paramount.

Cities like Rotterdam are pioneering efforts in this space, utilizing data to simulate and prepare for extreme weather events. By mapping vulnerabilities and crafting dynamic response strategies, cities can mitigate the impacts of floods, heatwaves, and other natural hazards, safeguarding both infrastructure and citizen well-being.

The Symphony of Data in Future Cities

Data-driven urban management represents a transformative approach to city life, one where data is as valuable as any tangible resource. This shift requires a symbiotic relationship between technology and governance, one that embraces change while grounding it in ethical practices.

162

As cities continue to grow and evolve, the harmony of data-driven management will become increasingly vital, orchestrating a carefully balanced urban ecosystem. Through innovative applications and responsive strategies, data will continue to enhance city operations, making urban spaces not just places to live, but places to thrive. This symphony is, indeed, the music of future cities, resonating with notes of efficiency, equity, and environmental stewardship.

9.4 Role of AI and IoT in Urban Sustainability

In the future of urban sustainability, a powerful alliance is forming—one driven by the remarkable potential of Artificial Intelligence (AI) and the Internet of Things (IoT). These technologies are rapidly becoming the cornerstone of smart cities, introducing unprecedented ways to manage resources, enhance city living, and reduce our carbon footprint. Imagine a city that thinks and communicates seamlessly with itself, anticipating the needs of its citizens and responding to environmental challenges in real time. This is not a scene from a sci-fi movie, but rather the evolution of our urban environment.

The Intelligence Behind AI in Urban Contexts

At the heart of this transformation lies AI, an ingenious tool tailored for processing and analyzing vast amounts of data more swiftly and accurately than any human task force. AI systems excel at recognizing patterns, predicting outcomes, and optimizing processes, making them invaluable for addressing the complex challenges faced by urban planners.

In traffic management, for instance, AI algorithms can

adjust traffic signals dynamically—not just to ease congestion, but to reduce emissions by minimizing idling time. Paris has successfully implemented AI-driven traffic control systems that have significantly improved traffic flow while enhancing air quality.

Moreover, AI contributes to urban energy management by fine-tuning the operation of smart grids. By forecasting energy demand and efficiently allocating resources, AI helps cities like Seoul balance their energy loads, integrate renewable sources, and avoid blackouts, all while diminishing their carbon footprint.

IoT: The Sentient Network

If AI provides the intelligence, IoT forms the sensory grid.   IoT links various urban elements through a network of sensors and devices, allowing them to communicate and collaborate.   This network feeds AI systems with the real-time data needed to make informed decisions, akin to providing eyes and ears to a strategic brain.

Consider the humble streetlamp, which, in a smart city, is no longer just a light source.   In cities like San Diego, streetlamps are equipped with sensors that monitor humidity, temperature, and even gunshot occurrences, while adaptive lighting reduces energy usage when fewer people are around.   This twofold approach conserves energy and enhances public safety.

On a broader scale, Amsterdam's water management system leverages over 12,000 IoT sensors, which continuously monitor water levels and pump activity. This smart water grid allows precise control and predictive management, significantly reducing the risk of both flooding and resource overuse.

The Intersection of AI, IoT, and Sustainability

When AI and IoT technologies converge, the result is a dynamic interplay that can dramatically enhance urban sustainability initiatives. For instance, in reducing waste, these technologies streamline municipal operations by accurately predicting service needs. Smart waste collection systems analyze fill levels in garbage bins to optimize collection routes, saving fuel and labor while maintaining cleaner streets.

Rio de Janeiro offers a vivid case in point with its urban operations center, where AI and IoT merge to monitor urban metrics ranging from crime rates to environmental conditions. By predicting weather patterns and anticipating natural disasters, the city's emergency response is not only agile but precise—an effective measure in mitigating disaster impacts and enhancing urban resilience.

Smart Urban Planning and Citizen Engagement

The implications of this technological symbiosis extend beyond infrastructure to urban planning and community engagement. By providing city planners with insights derived from data analytics, AI and IoT facilitate more informed decisions about future developments, zoning laws, and environmental impact assessments.

Citizen engagement is another vital dimension. Smart city platforms empower residents to participate in governance, providing feedback through apps and interactive dashboards. In Barcelona, citizens can influence decisions on urban projects by interacting directly with the city's data portal, ensuring governance that reflects community needs and aspirations.

Ethical Considerations and Accessibility

However, as with all transformative technologies, ethical considerations loom large. Privacy issues are at the forefront, as AI and IoT rely on collecting vast amounts of data. Cities must ensure data protection and transparency to maintain public trust, crafting regulations that safeguard citizens' privacy while enabling technological advancement.

Accessibility is another critical area. Efforts must be taken to ensure equitable access to smart city benefits, preventing technology from becoming a source of inequality. This involves not only providing digital access across diverse populations but also fostering digital literacy to fully integrate all citizens into the urban technological ecosystem.

A Gateway to Smart, Sustainable Futures

The role of AI and IoT in urban sustainability unfolds as a narrative of possibility—one where cities can preemptively tackle issues long before they manifest as crises. By weaving intelligence into the very fabric of urban operations, these technologies offer a future where cities are not just places to survive, but thriving ecosystems that prioritize environmental stewardship and human well being.

As this narrative progresses, the fusion of AI and IoT becomes more than a catalyst for change; it serves as a gateway to a new era in urban living. In embracing these technologies, cities are not just evolving—they are transforming into smart, sustainable beacons that beckon toward a more promising horizon. The promise of AI and IoT is not merely in their potential to innovate, but in their profound ability to redefine what the urban future can be: responsive, responsible, and undeniably regenerative.

9.5 Challenges and Ethics of Urban Technology Adoption

As cities worldwide embrace the allure of technology to enhance urban living, a tapestry of ethical considerations and challenges unfurls. While technology promises smarter, more efficient cities, its adoption is beset with complexities that extend beyond engineering marvels into the realms of human rights, privacy, and equity.

Urban technology adoption is not just about implementing advanced systems; it demands a conscientious approach that respects the social contracts and ethical frameworks within urban landscapes. As we plunge into these multifaceted issues, it becomes clear that technology is a powerful tool that requires careful stewardship and thoughtful integration into the urban ecosystem.

Privacy Concerns: The Invisible Observer

Imagine a city outfitted with a web of sensors, cameras, and data analytics platforms, continuously collecting information to optimize urban life. While this paints a picture of efficiency, it also raises pressing privacy concerns. The surveillance capabilities of smart cities can feel like a scene from George Orwell's dystopian tale, where the line between benign monitoring and invasive surveillance is perilously thin.

The deployment of facial recognition technology in public spaces, as seen in cities like San Francisco, has sparked debates over privacy rights and the potential for misuse. The ethical dilemma here pivots on the need for security and the right to privacy. Transparent governance frameworks and robust data protection policies are imperative to maintaining this delicate balance, ensuring citizens

167

retain control over their personal information.

The Digital Divide: Bridging the Gap

While technology offers solutions to urban challenges, an underlying issue is its accessibility—or rather, the lack thereof. The digital divide refers to the gap between those with easy access to digital technologies and those without. This divide can exacerbate existing inequalities, leaving marginalized communities behind as cities march toward digital futures.

Consider the case of internet access variability, where residents of affluent areas enjoy high-speed connectivity while others struggle with unreliable networks. Singapore addresses this by prioritizing digital inclusion initiatives, ensuring that all residents can participate in the digital economy. The ethical mandate is clear: as technology evolves, so must the commitment to universal accessibility, creating inclusive urban environments that benefit all citizens.

Data Governance: The Custodianship of Information

In the era of big data, cities find themselves in possession of vast repositories of information. The question then arises: who owns this data, and how should it be managed? Data governance becomes crucial in establishing the rules of the road for urban technology use, as seen in Toronto's smart city project, Quayside.

Controversy erupted when discussions of data ownership and management sparked fears of corporate overreach and insufficient public oversight. The episode underscored the importance of establishing clear policies regarding data custodianship, where the focus shifts to ensuring data serves the public interest and is safeguarded against exploitation.

Ethical AI: A Conundrum of Bias

Artificial Intelligence, hailed as a cornerstone of smart city infrastructure, presents its own ethical challenges. Algorithms can inadvertently reinforce societal biases, as they are often trained on historical data that may not accurately reflect current values. This bias can manifest in AI-driven systems like predictive policing, as seen in some U.S. cities, raising concerns about fairness and discrimination.

To combat this, transparency in AI development and implementation is essential. Efforts must focus on creating ethical AI practices that promote fairness, accountability, and inclusivity, reshaping systems that are genuinely equitable and just.

Technological Dependency: The Fragile City

An often-overlooked challenge is the city's increasing dependency on technology, creating vulnerabilities to cyber-attacks and system failures. A city reliant on digital systems for crucial services can face cascading effects if networks collapse or are compromised.

Consider the urban havoc caused by ransomware attacks on municipal infrastructure, such as the 2019 cyberattack on Baltimore's city government. Such incidents highlight the necessity for resilient and secure technological frameworks. Ensuring redundancy, investing in cybersecurity, and fostering a culture of technology mindfulness are vital in safeguarding urban resilience.

Ethical Implementation: A Collaborative Endeavor

Ultimately, the successful and ethical adoption of technology in cities is a collaborative effort. Stakeholders, including governments, the private sector, and citizens, must engage in dialogue and decision-making processes, embodying a spirit of

co-creation.   Policies must embody ethical principles
enshrined in human rights, ensuring that the benefits of
technology are equitably shared across society.

Examples of participatory urban planning can be
observed in cities like Helsinki, where residents are
involved in the co-design of urban projects through
online platforms and community workshops.   Such
inclusive approaches ensure the diverse needs of
citizens are met while fostering trust and accountability.

A Balanced Path Forward

Navigating the ethical labyrinth of urban technology
adoption demands thoughtful consideration and
proactive management.   While technology offers
powerful solutions to urban challenges, its integration
must prioritize the human dimension.   As cities evolve,
the ethical frameworks guiding this transformation
must keep pace, embodying fairness, transparency, and
inclusivity.

Technology's role in urban sustainability is not just about
advancing infrastructure but enhancing the very fabric
of urban society.   By embracing these ethical considerations, cities can craft futures that are not only smarter but
also more just and compassionate. Engaging with these
challenges presents a unique opportunity to build urban
environments that reflect our highest values, ensuring
that technological progress is a force for good shared by
all.

Chapter 10

Policy and Governance for Sustainable Urban Development

This chapter focuses on the frameworks and governance models essential for sustainable urban development. It highlights the role of public-private partnerships and community involvement in policymaking. By addressing challenges in policy implementation, it underscores the importance of effective, inclusive governance in driving sustainability initiatives, ensuring compliance, and aligning urban development with ecological and social objectives for long-term resilience.

10.1 Frameworks for Sustainable Urban Policies

When discussing sustainable urban development, it is imperative to consider the frameworks that guide the creation of effective policies. These frameworks act as blueprints, helping cities navigate the complex terrain of sustainability by aligning economic growth, social welfare, and environmental health. Understanding them reveals how local governments, urban planners, and com-

munities can work together to foster cities that are not
only livable but also resilient to the challenges of the future.

At the heart of any sustainable urban policy framework is
the principle of balance—one that encourages a holistic
integration of varied sectoral plans: transport, housing,
energy, and waste management, to name a few. The
World Commission on Environment and Development's
1987 Brundtland Report was a pivotal moment, defining sustainable development as a means of meeting "the
needs of the present without compromising the ability
of future generations to meet their own needs." This report laid down the moral and ethical groundwork for numerous frameworks developed thereafter, all driving towards sustainability's triple bottom line—people, planet,
and prosperity.

One of the most significant international frameworks
is the United Nations' Sustainable Development
Goals (SDGs), particularly Goal 11, which calls
for making cities inclusive, safe, resilient, and
sustainable. This goal encompasses aspects such as
affordable housing, sustainable transport systems,
and participatory planning, stressing the importance
of a comprehensive strategy. The SDGs serve as a
guiding light; however, their broad nature necessitates
more localized frameworks to address specific urban
challenges.

Enter the realm of Local Agenda 21. Stemming from the
Earth Summit in Rio de Janeiro in 1992, Local Agenda 21
encouraged local governments to create and implement
their sustainable development plans with active
community engagement. Here, the emphasis was on
tailoring solutions to fit the unique cultural, economic,
and environmental circumstances of individual cities.
This framework not only brought sustainability down

172

to a manageable, local scale but also highlighted the importance of community voices in decision-making processes—a theme we'll explore further in subsequent sections.

A practical application of Agenda 21 can be seen in successful cases such as Curitiba, Brazil. Often heralded as a model for sustainable urban planning, Curitiba's initiatives include an innovative bus rapid transit system and extensive green spaces, all set within a framework that prioritized ecological and social equity long before these became mainstream urban buzzwords.

Parallel to this, the C40 Cities Climate Leadership Group offers another sound example of a voluntary framework promoting collaborative learning and policy adoption among major cities. It focuses on reducing greenhouse gas emissions and climate risks, fostering a peer-to-peer network where cities can share successes and challenges. This framework is a testament to the power of shared goals and cooperation in scaling effective policy measures across disparate urban landscapes.

On a policy level, frameworks like Smart Growth encourage the development of compact, walkable city centers that reduce car dependency. By promoting mixed land uses and transportation options, Smart Growth seeks to improve quality of life and preserve the natural environment. This approach illustrates a shift from the sprawling urban development patterns of the 20th century, emphasizing sustainable regional planning.

In addition to the international frameworks, it is crucial to acknowledge the role of national and regional policies that align with sustainable urban objectives. For instance, the European Green Capital Award outlines criteria for urban environmental sustainability, incentivizing cities to innovate and improve their ecological credentials. National frameworks allow for the creation of standardized metrics and benchmarks, offering a coherent structure for cities to work within and meet sustainability targets.

Yet, with all these frameworks, the challenge remains to measure progress accurately. This is where tools like environmental impact assessments (EIA) and sustainability indicators become indispensable. By ensuring that urban projects align with these frameworks both in planning and execution, policymakers can verify their impact and make adjustments as needed.

However, let's not forget one essential ingredient in this mix—flexibility. Urban environments are dynamic, and so our frameworks must allow for adaptability to emerging technologies, shifting demographics, and unexpected challenges, such as those posed by the global pandemic. Flexibility ensures that while the frameworks are robust, they do not become outdated in the face of novelty or adversity.

The journey towards sustainable urban development is a long one, and while frameworks provide the roadmap, commitment from all stakeholders—government, private sector, and citizens alike—is needed to follow it through. By adhering to these guiding structures, cities can transition from theoretical ambitions of sustainability into practical, everyday realities—transforming urban spaces into thriving ecosystems that serve both current inhabitants and future generations alike.

10.2 Governance Models for Effective Implementation

At the heart of any successful sustainable urban initiative lies a robust governance model. Governance in this context refers to the structures and processes that allow cities to manage resources, execute policies, and coordinate among diverse stakeholders. Effective governance is essential in turning the theoretical frameworks we explored previously into practical action, ensuring cities are not just planned for sustainability but are lived as sustainable spaces.

In considering governance models, it is critical to appreciate the complexity of urban systems. Cities are intricate entities composed of myriad interconnected components: economic systems, social networks, infrastructures, and natural environments. Thus, governance models must be adaptable, inclusive, and multifaceted to address the wide array of challenges cities face today.

To begin, let us examine the centralized governance model. Traditionally, many cities have relied on a top-down approach where decision-making resides with a central authority, such as a city council or municipal government. This model provides a clear chain of command and can be efficient for implementing policies swiftly. Historical examples include the massive infrastructural projects of the mid-20th century, like the construction of interstate highway systems in the United States, which were largely executed through centralized decision-making.

While effective for certain large-scale initiatives, centralized models often struggle with issues of inclusivity and local responsiveness. They can lead to policies that lack

175

the nuance needed to address localized environmental, social, and economic contexts. As a result, there has been a shift towards more decentralized governance models, favoring greater local autonomy and participatory approaches.

Decentralized governance advocates for distributing decision-making powers across various layers of government and directly involving local stakeholders. This model is about empowering communities, recognizing the value of local knowledge, and fostering stakeholder engagement in the policy-making process. Cities like Portland, Oregon, are noted for their decentralized governance, where neighborhood associations play an integral role in shaping city policies, leading to more tailored and accepted sustainability initiatives.

A pertinent example can be observed in the transformation of Medellín, Colombia. Once infamous for its crime rates, Medellín underwent a remarkable urban renaissance through innovative governance. By fostering collaboration between the local government, private sector, and community groups, Medellín developed a series of social urbanism projects, including urban staircases and libraries, effectively integrating marginalized communities into the city's fabric. This participatory governance model has turned Medellín into a beacon of urban transformation and sustainability.

Another governance approach gaining traction is network governance. In this model, governance is not merely about the public sector but involves horizontal collaboration across governments, the private sector, non-profits, and civil society. It leverages the strengths of diverse actors to create synergies, fostering more resilient and innovative solutions. The C40 Cities Climate Leadership Group is an example where cities share best practices and collaborate on climate change initiatives, demonstrating the potential of network governance in achieving urban sustainability goals.

The importance of intergovernmental collaboration cannot be overstated in understanding governance models. The challenges cities face—climate change, immigration, economic inequality—often transcend municipal boundaries, requiring regional or even global coordination. Metropolitan governance, which encompasses collaboration across cities within a larger urban area, is instrumental in managing shared resources such as water systems, transportation networks, and air quality.

An illustrative case is that of Greater Manchester in the UK, which has adopted a combined authority governance model. Here, ten municipalities coordinate on cross-cutting issues like economic development and transportation, enhancing regional coherence while allowing for localized social and environmental strategies. This regional model strikes a balance between the need for overarching strategic plans and the specificity of local implementation.

Nevertheless, governance models must be dynamic to meet the shifting sands of urban challenges. Adaptive governance focuses on learning and experimentation, encouraging cities to be laboratories for sustainability efforts. This approach values feedback loops, monitoring, and continuous improvement, akin to the iterative process of scientific discovery.

Challenges such as the COVID-19 pandemic have underscored the necessity for flexible governance models that can rapidly adapt to unforeseen crises. Many cities have demonstrated this adaptability, reimagining public spaces as pedestrian areas or bike lanes to accommodate social distancing while promoting sustainable transport.

Ultimately, the effectiveness of urban governance models hinges on accountability and transparency. Citizens must have confidence that governance structures are fair, equitable, and prioritize the common good. Engaging citizens not just as passive beneficiaries but as active co-creators in urban sustainability efforts is crucial.

While no one-size-fits-all governance model exists, cities that blend elements from various approaches tend to navigate the complexities of sustainable urban development most effectively. By coordinating effort, stakeholders, and resources through innovative governance models, today's cities have the potential to chart a course towards a sustainable and vibrant urban future—one where the spaces we inhabit flourish not despite us, but because of the thoughtful, inclusive, and purposeful stewardship we provide.

10.3   Role of Public-Private Partnerships

In the quest for sustainable cities, one cannot overlook the transformative potential of public-private partnerships (PPPs). These partnerships are the proverbial meeting of minds where public ambitions intertwine with private pragmatism, creating a synergy that often results in innovative solutions to urban challenges. But what exactly makes PPPs so effective, and why are they a key component of sustainable urban development?

To understand the prominence of PPPs, let us take a brief stroll down memory lane. Historically, urban development was primarily the domain of public authorities, with governments shouldering the lion's share of planning and execution. However, as cities expanded and their problems multiplied, it became evident that relying solely on public resources and capabilities was neither feasible nor efficient. Enter the private sector, with its capital, efficiency, and innovative prowess.

PPPs emerged as a concerted effort to harness the strengths of both sectors, aligning the public sector's mandate to serve societal needs with the profit-driven efficiency of private businesses. This marriage became vital when addressing the multi-dimensional nature of sustainability—balancing environmental protection, social equity, and economic viability.

One of the defining features of successful PPPs is risk-sharing. Urban projects, notably those linked to infrastructure—be it transportation, waste management, or energy systems—often involve substantial financial and operational risks. By distributing these risks between public and private partners, PPPs not only reduce the burden on each party but also foster a spirit of collaboration and mutual accountability.

Take, for instance, the celebrated example of London's congestion charge system. Introduced as a means to reduce traffic and pollution, this project was underpinned by a PPP that combined government oversight with private technological expertise and investment. The initiative led to a marked decrease in congestion and a boost in public transport use, illustrating how PPPs can effectively drive urban sustainability.

Beyond transportation, PPPs are increasingly penetrating the green energy sector. Cities around the world are forming alliances with private energy companies to transition towards renewable sources. A notable instance is

179

the city of San Diego, which partnered with private firms to advance its aim of running entirely on renewable energy by 2035. This partnership not only accelerates the city's sustainability goals but also stimulates local economic growth by fostering innovation and creating jobs within the clean energy sector.

It is also fascinating to observe how PPPs facilitate technological integration in urban landscapes. The modernization of city services through smart technologies often requires significant upfront investment—something that the private sector is generally more equipped to provide. Smart grids, intelligent waste management systems, and data-driven public safety networks have all benefited from PPPs that leverage private-sector technology and innovation under the regulatory frameworks set by public authorities.

PPPs are not without their challenges, however. They require clear agreements and robust governance frameworks to ensure that partnerships genuinely serve the public interest and do not succumb to the pitfalls of profit-driven motivations at the expense of societal well-being. Transparency, as previously mentioned in our discussion on governance models, plays a crucial role here. It is essential for PPP contracts to be transparent and include well-defined performance metrics, enabling effective public oversight.

The cultural dimensions of PPPs also bear consideration. Societal attitudes towards private involvement in public services can vary significantly from one region to another. In societies with a strong public service ethos, for example, there is often skepticism around the privatization of services traditionally managed by governmental bodies. It is crucial for PPPs in these contexts to cultivate trust by ensuring public values are safeguarded.

On a broader scale, international collaborations facilitated through PPPs are pivotal in tackling urban sustainability challenges. Initiatives such as the Global Infrastructure Hub, developed by the G20 countries, demonstrate how pooling resources and expertise across borders can catalyze sustainable infrastructure development worldwide. Such partnerships transcend local capacities, providing global visions and solutions to the intricate challenges of urbanization and climate change.

Moreover, PPPs can bolster local capacity-building, transferring knowledge and skills from established industries to local government administrations. This not only enhances the immediate success of sustainability projects but also augments the long-term capability of municipalities to manage and maintain such projects independently.

From conceptualizing innovative city spaces to implementing cutting-edge environmental measures, PPPs remain an indispensable tool in the urban planner's kit, providing a flexible but structured framework to meet the dynamic needs of cities today. In a rapidly urbanizing world, their role in fostering sustainable, livable cities continues to grow, underlining the potential for human ingenuity when collaboration supersedes competition.

As we look towards the future, the adaptability of PPPs suggests that they will remain central to reimagining urban living. The goal is for cities to evolve not merely as agglomerations of buildings and roads but as vibrant ecosystems, nurtured through partnerships that blend public aspirations with private sector dynamism. In this dance of collaboration, cities stand to gain significantly, fostering environments that are as sustainable as they are innovative.

10.4   Community Involvement in Policy Making

When it comes to building sustainable cities, there's a common phrase that rings true: the whole is greater than the sum of its parts. Nowhere is this more apparent than in the critical role of community involvement in the policy-making process. Communities are not just passive recipients of urban policies; they are active architects of their environments, possessing the insight and motivation to drive meaningful and lasting change. Thus, engaging the community is not simply a box to tick in sustainable development—it is the very cornerstone of it.

Historically, many urban policies came from a top-down approach, where decisions were made by a select few behind closed doors. While this might have ensured swift decision-making, it often resulted in policies that were out of touch with the needs and aspirations of the people they were meant to serve. As cities burgeoned in size and complexity, this disconnect only grew starker.

Enter the era of participatory governance. This paradigm shift encouraged city planners and policy-makers to open the doors, quite literally, to community input and participation. A sense of agency among community members creates policies that are not only more reflective of real needs but also enhance public trust and accountability. After all, who better understands the pulse of a city than its own residents?

The concept of participatory governance isn't just theoretical—it has roots in concrete successes around the globe. One illustrative example is the participatory budgeting process initiated in Porto Alegre, Brazil, in the late 1980s. Here, community residents were given control over the allocation of a portion of the municipal budget. The process democratized decision-making, and the results were transformative; improved public services, greater transparency, and a burgeoning civic spirit demonstrated the model's potential.

In community involvement, diversity of perspective is invaluable. Urban populations are not monolithic; they comprise people from varied backgrounds, each contributing unique experiences and needs. Ensuring equitable representation in policy-making can bridge gaps and foster social cohesion by systematically addressing issues that different groups face. For instance, involving marginalized communities—who are often the most affected by unsustainable practices—can lead to policies prioritizing environmental justice, housing affordability, and equitable access to services.

Yet, fostering genuine community involvement is not without its challenges. One key obstacle is overcoming the traditional power dynamics and skepticism of those who have felt historically unheard or excluded. Building trust takes time and effort, demanding transparency and consistency from policymakers. Techniques such as town hall meetings, community workshops, and digital platforms for feedback can be instrumental, provided they are designed to be inclusive and accessible to all segments of the community.

An interesting case study is found in the City of Barcelona, where digital participation platforms, like Decidim, have empowered citizens to propose, debate, and vote on policy initiatives. This technological bridge connects citizens and city officials in real time, making policy-making a continuous and adaptable process rather than a periodic task.

Moreover, fostering a culture of lifelong civic engagement is vital. It isn't just about drawing in participants for a single initiative but cultivating an environment where community members are consistently engaged and invested in the process. Education plays a pivotal role here, starting from school curriculums that emphasize active citizenship and continuing with adult education programs that inform residents about their role and rights in shaping urban policy.

Sustainable urban policy isn't just about creating the right infrastructure or enacting strict regulations; it is also about nurturing an environment where people feel empowered to contribute and effect change. By investing in these resources, cities can create an informed citizenry ready to tackle sustainability challenges.

It is crucial to measure and evaluate the impact of community involvement. Many cities employ participatory metrics to assess community engagement outcomes, ensuring that the involvement is not merely perfunctory but genuinely influences decisions. These metrics offer feedback loops, guiding future policy frameworks to be even more inclusive and responsive.

Community involvement in policy-making holds a unique and transformative power, serving as a vital pivot towards more sustainable, inclusive, and resilient urban environments. By melding the wisdom of residents with the technical know-how of planners and policymakers, cities can sculpt futures that are not only more sustainable but also enrich the quality of life for all inhabitants. This reciprocal relationship makes every stakeholder a custodian of the city's legacy, encouraging an urban development model built not just for the people but by them. As cities worldwide continue to grow and evolve, embracing community involvement isn't merely an option—it is the blueprint for forging urban landscapes in which the ethos of sustainability thrives.

10.5 Challenges in Policy Implementation and Compliance

If designing policies for sustainable urban development is akin to drafting the blueprint for a grand edifice, then implementing these policies is the Herculean task of actual construction. The path from policymaking to execution and compliance is fraught with obstacles, each more daunting than the last, yet none insurmountable. Understanding these challenges can provide the insights necessary for overcoming them, ensuring that the vision of sustainable cities becomes a lived reality.

One of the most significant hurdles in policy implementation is the notorious gap between formulation and execution—a chasm where well-intentioned plans often languish. This gap can arise from several factors, beginning with the disjointed communication between policymakers and implementers. In many cases, policies are crafted with broad strokes, lacking the granularity needed by those "in the trenches" tasked with their execution. Clear instructions, precise objectives, and adaptable frameworks are essential to bridge this divide, ensuring that implementers have both the directive and the freedom to adapt policies to specific contexts.

For example, consider the ambitious environmental policies seen in major urban centers like New York City's plan to transform its waste management system. The execution of such policies requires not just an operational understanding but an alignment with local sanitation departments and private waste companies, who must be brought on board early in the planning process to provide their insights and address logistical concerns.

185

Funding is another stumbling block, often turning grand urban visions into empty promises. Even the most meticulously designed policies require financial backing for implementation, yet urban budgets are often constrained by competing demands. Effective policy execution and compliance thus necessitate innovative financing solutions. Public-private partnerships, which we've detailed earlier, play a crucial role here, marrying public objectives with private capital to ensure that projects have the financial foundation they need to succeed.

Additionally, fostering a culture of compliance is paramount. No policy can be effective if it is consistently ignored or circumvented. Ensuring compliance often involves a blend of incentives and enforcement. Urban policies must be structured in such a way that compliance becomes the path of least resistance, while also dangling the carrot of positive reinforcement, such as tax incentives or public recognition, to encourage adherence.

Singapore serves as a fascinating case study in achieving high levels of compliance, particularly in environmental policies. Through a combination of strict regulations, public education campaigns, and compliance incentives—like reduced vehicle taxes for environmentally friendly cars—Singapore has succeeded in significantly reducing emissions and pollution levels. This model of coupling enforcement with incentives provides valuable lessons for cities grappling with similar challenges.

An often overlooked but critical component of successful policy implementation is the element of time. Urban policy changes require patience and gradual implementation to allow stakeholders to adapt. Rapid changes can be met with resistance, especially if they disrupt exist-

186

ing systems or threaten established interests. Phased implementation plans with clearly defined milestones and timelines can help ease the transition for communities, businesses, and public entities alike.

Furthermore, the pursuit of effective policy implementation must account for technological evolution and the data they produce—assets central to monitoring compliance and measuring success. Smart technologies and data analytics are indispensable for offering real-time insights into how policies perform and where adjustments are necessary. However, it is crucial to approach this with a privacy-conscious mindset, ensuring that data collection does not infringe upon individual rights.

An inspiring example is the use of data in Copenhagen, where city officials monitor environmental data to adjust climate policies dynamically. This adaptive management approach ensures that policies remain relevant and effective over time, offering a responsive model that can be replicated in other metropolises.

The obstacles to effective policy implementation and compliance in urban environments are as varied as they are challenging, yet they are not insurmountable. By acknowledging these challenges and embracing strategies that include collaborative engagement, robust financing, phased operations, and adaptive management, cities can transform their sustainable policy aspirations into actions. This transformative process is essential as cities strive to meet the needs of today while preserving resources and opportunities for future generations—a delicate balancing act that demands both vigilance and vision.